MINISTRY at the MARGINS

The Prophetic Mission of Women, Youth & the Poor

Cheryl J. Sanders

WIPF & STOCK · Eugene, Oregon

Wipf and Stock Publishers
199 W 8th Ave, Suite 3
Eugene, OR 97401

Ministry at the Margins
The Prophetic Mission of Women, Youth & the Poor
By Sanders, Cheryl J.
Copyright©1997 by Sanders, Cheryl J.
ISBN 13: 978-1-60608-760-2
Publication date 5/1/2009
Previously published by Intervarsity Press, 1997

For my parents
Doris Haizlip Sanders
and Wallace Sanders Jr.
with love and appreciation

ACKNOWLEDGMENTS   *9*

INTRODUCTION   *11*

PART I   THE ETHICS OF THE GOSPEL: *MINISTRY & MISSION*   *19*

1 ACCOUNTABILITY: *The Fear of the Lord*   *21*

2 COMPASSION: *The Kingdom Mandate*   *27*

3 EMPATHY: *The Golden Rule*   *35*

PART II   THE PROPHETIC MINISTRY OF WOMEN   *41*

4 MOTHERHOOD & REDEMPTION   *43*

5 THE PROPHETIC INITIATIVE   *52*

6 LETTING THE SPIRIT LEAD: *The Prophetic Witness of Women
in the Upper Room*   *57*

PART III   MINISTRY AT THE MARGINS: *CHILDREN & YOUTH*   *63*

7 PROPHETIC PARENTING   *65*

8 YOUR SONS & DAUGHTERS SHALL PROPHESY   *73*

9 EMPOWERING THE NEXT GENERATION   *79*

**PART IV   BREAKING DOWN BARRIERS: *A CHALLENGE
TO THE CHURCH***   *85*

10 THE CHILDREN'S BREAD   *87*

11 RECONCILIATION: *Jesus at Jericho*   *92*

12 MINISTRY & MISSION IN MULTICULTURAL PERSPECTIVE   *97*

EPILOGUE *Urban Ministry & Prophetic Mission:*
The Autobiography of Reverend Hattie Downer   *105*

SUGGESTIONS FOR FURTHER READING   *143*

Acknowledgments

There are many people who have helped me to bring my ministry and scholarship to voice in these pages. I must first acknowledge the significant part my family has played in my life over the years. I have dedicated the book to my parents, Wallace and Doris Sanders, whose loving care created a wonderful environment for my spiritual and professional formation. I owe my dear husband, Alan Carswell, a debt of gratitude for his stellar commitment to a quality of partnership that has helped me to balance a full schedule of teaching, pastoring, writing and travel with the priority of maintaining a Christian household for ourselves and our two children, Allison and Garrett.

I cherish Reverend Hattie Downer's courageous example of how to do ministry "at the margins." She has nurtured many ministers and lay leaders in the Church of God, and I am pleased to have the opportunity to share her story with a wider audience.

I am encouraged in this work by my day-to-day interactions with students and faculty colleagues at Howard University, and by the kind hospitality I have received as preacher and lecturer at Anderson University and on other Christian college campuses too numerous to name here. In addition, this book is enriched by the blessing of fruitful dialogue with evangelical Christian intellectuals who have the courage to connect critical thinking with fervent faith, including my editor, Rodney Clapp, and Curtiss DeYoung, Craig Keener, Charles Marsh, A. G. Miller, Bill Pannell, Eugene Rivers, J. Deotis Roberts,

John and Susie Stanley, Harold Dean Trulear and David Whettstone.

Finally, I am grateful for the Third Street Church of God, which has provided a spiritual home for four generations of my family, including the Haizlips, the Sanders and the Carswells. This congregation has exemplified and embodied the central concerns of this book on several levels, as a place where the prophetic ministry of both women and men can be affirmed, where children and youth are viewed as a significant focus of urban mission, and where meaningful relationships are established daily with the poor of the streets and shelters of Washington. The late Dr. Samuel George Hines (1929-1995) devoted his twenty-five years of pastoral leadership at Third Street Church to the ministry of reconciliation across the barriers of race and class. It is hoped that this book will further his legacy of fostering Christian unity by providing an honest assessment of what it will take to bring the ministry at the margins to the center of attention in the body of Christ.

INTRODUCTION

SF -
C $\overline{\text{M}}$ -
   M -
   C -

This book is an interpretation of prophetic ministry in the Bible as understood from the vantage point of the "margins," that is, the disadvantaged position of women, children and the poor in contemporary society. This process begins with an examination of the Scriptures to discover what roles women, children and the poor played in the ministry and mission of Jesus Christ. An important assumption guiding the explication and application of the gospel here is the view that Jesus centered his proclamation of the good news in the life situation of the marginalized people of his day. It is clear that Jesus gave priority to the ethical principles of justice and love in his interactions with others. However, his ethical teachings and practices drew a better response from the multitudes than from the elite. Indeed, his call to discipleship was largely rejected by the rich and the religious, and his claims concerning the kingdom of God did not cater to the special interests of the powerful and the privileged. The people on the margins of society celebrated his ministry among them, while those identified with the centers of religious and imperial power joined forces to crucify him.

In Matthew 23:23 Jesus rebukes the religious elite for attending to the detail of the law without addressing the most important things

What is the prophetic mandate

the law requires: "Woe to you, scribes and Pharisees, hypocrites! For you tithe mint, dill, and cummin, and have neglected the weightier matters of the law: justice and mercy and faith. It is these you ought to have practiced without neglecting the others." There are liberal "scribes" and conservative "Pharisees" in our evangelical churches today—those who follow the liberal line that it is the government's responsibility to increase the life opportunities of minorities, women and the poor, and those who follow the conservative line that one's life's fortunes ought to be solely determined by individual initiative. The former fail to recognize that all the programs in the world will not improve the condition of a person or family that lacks motivation for moral and economic advancement. The latter fail to recognize that in the real world everybody who is successful depends on the mercy and graces of others, and especially within the corridors of political and economic power, where "old boy" networks still are the principal means of white male access even at entry level. But as long as the network is in place and unchanged except by the admission of a few token "others," then justice and equality are held at bay.

One way of resolving this dichotomy politically is to advocate a moderate evangelical perspective which gives full and fruitful expression to the prophetic mandate in the public arena with integrity. This prophetic mandate cannot be seen as inherently "conservative," because it calls for repentance and structural change; at the same time it cannot be identified as inherently "liberal," because it appeals to traditional values with reference to the love and justice of God. Instead of aligning ourselves uncritically with the "right" or "left," evangelical moderates can be guided in our political decision-making by three specific virtues: the courage to confront even the most deeply entrenched evils of society, the wisdom to develop constructive alternatives and strategies to rectify past injustices and promote a just future, and the compassion to bring about reconciliation and human wholeness wherever possible.

3 virtues

Can modern evangelical Christians summon the resolve to repent of past sins and become converted to the truth that promises to set *we must unmask the untruthfulness of this system.*

us all free? Racism and sexism thrive on the perpetuation of lies about the relative worth and abilities of human beings, based on misconceptions concerning the impact of skin color and sex on human outcomes. The Christian prophetic imperative is to unmask the untruthfulness of this system. The root of the evils of racism and sexism is the desire to dominate—and this desire can afflict anyone regardless of race, sex or class. If we can deal with this lust for domination on a personal level as sin, and work toward elimination of the social structures that have been erected by persons and groups in the service of their own interests to the exclusion of others (even to the extreme of denying the humanity of others, as in the institution of slavery), then we can create a fruitful connection between our Christian confession and our social consciousness.

Q *to ask our selves* We must begin by making an honest assessment of where each of us stands within the status quo. Am I especially privileged or disadvantaged by the system? Or must I divest myself of the illusion of being unaffected by the system? How would my life circumstances change if I pursued justice in my own situation, practiced equity in my dealings with others, challenged injustice in my spheres of influence and advocated increased access and opportunities for others who have less than I do?

Jesus engaged the justice question at the heart of his teaching, preaching and healing, when he issued an invitation to the kingdom of God to all persons, male and female, Jew and Gentile, righteous and unrighteous. Similarly, Peter's personal biases were overruled by the Holy Spirit at the Gentile Pentecost, when he confessed the revelation that "God shows no partiality" (Acts 10:34), a confession at least as important as the one he made at Caesarea Philippi of Jesus as the Christ. This second Pentecost suggests that God has a way of bringing forth the same message repeatedly. After all, the initial Pentecost was a multicultural event, involving men and women of all nations in fulfillment of Joel's prophecy that a generation of "sons and daughters" would prophesy, but the church leaders did not get the message of inclusiveness the first time around. Some of us still don't get it.

"THE ROOT OF RACISM IS THE DESIRE TO DOMINATE AND THIS DESIRE CAN DOMINATE EVERYONE REGARDLESS OF RACE, SEX OR CLASS."

the second pentecost?

My purpose in writing this book is to reiterate this message and to underscore the need to awaken a deeper commitment to social justice among evangelical Christians. Ever since the time of slavery, evangelicals in the United States have been notorious for their sanctimonious complicity with the denial of the rights and well-being of various ethnic groups and women. And those Christians who have shown the most concern for justice issues in America have generally refrained from preaching or practicing a life-changing gospel. The ultimate objective of this study is to empower the church to embrace a fresh anointing to overcome evil with good by bringing evangelical faith and fervor into harness with an ethic of equality and justice for all, so that the ministry, mission and message of Christ can emerge into the third millennium with renewed authority and impact.

To analyze with honesty and integrity the interplay of race, sex, class and power in church and society remains one of the most pressing prophetic tasks to be undertaken by American Christians at the threshold of the twenty-first century. The theological, ethical and political concerns expressed thus far converge on one question: What relevance does the gospel of Jesus Christ have for women, children and the poor in a society where affluent white males have typically held exclusive control of goods, services and social policy? The chapters of this book are organized into four parts that address this question from the vantage point of the marginalized people whom Jesus embraced as he proclaimed the gospel of the kingdom of God: part I, "The Ethics of the Gospel: Ministry and Mission," part II, "The Prophetic Ministry of Women," part III, "Ministry at the Margins: Children and Youth," and part IV, "Breaking Down Barriers: A Challenge to the Church."

Part I outlines a basic ethical paradigm for interpreting the intent of ministry and mission in light of the gospel. Ethics, simply stated, is a system of moral reflection expressed in terms of principles and practices. The ethics of the gospel, or "gospel ethics," is a particular system of moral reflection, principles and practices embraced by persons who are committed to following the call and example of

Jesus Christ. The biblical foundation of gospel ethics is Jesus Christ's invitation for all people to experience God's righteousness as personal salvation and as social justice. Thus gospel ethics entails both witness and work—the witness of proclaiming the good news of God's reign in the world and the work of implementing righteousness and justice in people's lives. Justice is the moral principle that corresponds most closely to the divine attribute of righteousness. In ethical terms, justice is the imperative to do what is right in a manner that is fair and impartial. Ministry is service of God and humanity—to serve God obligates one to practice justice as it derives from God's nature and will. Similarly, the concept of mission, as understood in the literal sense of "sending" or "being sent," is inextricably linked with justice as both a primary motive for mission and an important measure of the effectiveness of mission.

The three chapters in part I address three ethical principles that enable the practical implementation of justice in the context of Christian ministry and mission. The chapter entitled "Accountability: The Fear of the Lord" lifts up the ethical principle of accountability, as expressed in the most basic axiom of the book of Proverbs, that "the fear of the LORD is the beginning of wisdom" (Prov 9:10). "Compassion: The Kingdom Mandate" deals with the ethics of compassion in mission as illustrated by the parable of the sheep and the goats, where eternal judgment is pronounced upon nations according to whether or not their sense of mission to the "least of these" manifests the same caring concern as would be offered to Christ himself. "Empathy: The Golden Rule" sets forth the principle of empathy with reference to the Golden Rule, Jesus' simple formula for practicing justice by first projecting oneself into the other person's shoes.

Part II, "The Prophetic Ministry of Women," examines the roles women have played in the redemption of fallen humanity, the unfolding of the ministry of Jesus and the mission of the New Testament church. Moreover, this section underscores the ethics of the gospel in light of the particular manner in which women have experienced divine empowerment in spite of their disadvantaged position in society. "Motherhood and Redemption" explains how two biblical mothers, Eve and Mary, embody God's plan for the redemption of humankind by means of the ministry and mission of motherhood. "The Prophetic Initiative" deals with the principle of authority in ministry, using the example of the woman who anointed Jesus at Bethany to illustrate prophetic ministry in action. Not only does this woman disciple take the initiative to anoint Jesus for his burial, but she also offers an informative illustration of how women who feel compelled to act with divine authority can deal with male opposition and denial. "Letting the Spirit Lead: The Prophetic Witness of Women in the Upper Room" demonstrates that the most important "act" of the first Christians in the book of Acts was to let the Spirit lead women and men together to do ministry with an enhanced awareness of God's righteousness and justice.

Part III, "Ministry at the Margins: Children and Youth," discusses the importance of children and youth as signifiers of the divine ethical intent as manifested in Christian ministry and mission at the margins. "Prophetic Parenting" examines the early spiritual formation of the child prophet Samuel under the guidance of Eli, an elderly priest whose own adult sons had defiled the temple with sexual and sacramental abuses. "Your Sons and Daughters Shall Prophesy" begins with a literal reading of Joel's prophecy as it finds fulfillment in the Pentecost event, implicating the practice of parenting as a special form of ministry that directs our children toward the fulfillment of divine justice. "Empowering the Next Generation" identifies young people in the early church who became witnesses of God's deliverance in instances of extreme distress.

The fourth and final part is "Breaking Down Barriers: A Challenge to the Church." The intent of this section is to challenge evangelical churches to embrace the multicultural scope and witness of the gospel with a genuine concern for justice. The fruit of such advocacy would be the renewed moral voice of a church that preaches what we practice, a twist on the familiar adage to practice what we preach. In other words, the church can attain the level of credibility needed for speaking prophetically to a deeply divided world only as we develop more concrete models and examples of how unity brings harmony to diversity within our own ranks. The contemporary church is urged to uphold biblical standards of justice in its ministry and mission by embracing the multicultural message of the gospel.

This part demonstrates from the perspective of gospel ethics several critical imperatives: to meet the challenge of diversity in the urban context, to share power without partiality and to manifest the unity of the church openly so the world may believe. "The Children's Bread" shows how a mother's sense of her child's urgent need causes her to confront Jesus and challenge him to extend the scope of his ministry and mission beyond the boundaries of religion and culture. When Jesus appears poised to withhold the blessing of healing from the Canaanite woman's daughter, she insists that he minister to her as a mother and as a Gentile. In "Reconciliation: Jesus at Jericho" the ministry of class and ethnic reconciliation in the urban context is illuminated based on the story of Zacchaeus, the healing of the blind man and the parable of the good Samaritan. "Ministry and Mission in Multicultural Perspective" examines the principle of empowerment in Peter's confession of Christ and in the conversion of Cornelius, revealing how and why power should be shared across barriers of race, sex and class. The chapter concludes with an exhortation to Christian unity based on an interpretation of Jesus' high-priestly prayer as recorded in the Gospel of John. This prayer communicates the universal message the gospel brings to bear on the world and prescribes for all believers the ethical task of making inclusivity work in God's church.

The epilogue is an oral history. The Reverend Hattie Downer of Brooklyn, New York, describes her work as Church of God pastor, urban missionary and national field worker for children and youth. Her story aptly incarnates the ministry concept presented in the preceding chapters.

The ethical perspectives set forth in this book were developed from sermons, lectures and conversations I have shared with my students at the Howard University School of Divinity and from the pulpit of Third Street Church of God, both in Washington, D.C., and also in the course of my visits to numerous churches, colleges and seminaries across America. I have been especially informed in this line of thinking by my participation in the prophetic ministry curriculum at Howard, which encourages students to bring critical theological and ethical reflection to their field work in urban settings where the special needs of women, children and the poor are being engaged through ministry and mission.

My calling is the ministry of the gospel of Jesus Christ. My full-time profession is as pastor, professor and parent to two children in partnership with my husband. The impact of these several roles on my ethical perspectives will readily be evident in the pages that follow. Because of who I am, I view the demands and challenges of ministry simultaneously from several vantage points—the parish, the academy and the family. Moreover, as an African-American woman I have no illusions about the pervasive effects of institutional racism, sexism and elitism both within and outside the church. My concern for justice is not purely academic—my burden for this book is to declare that the gospel of Jesus Christ coheres in the belief that a loving and just God has called all persons, from margin to center, "to do justice, and to love kindness, and to walk humbly with your God" (Mic 6:8).

PART I
THE ETHICS OF THE GOSPEL
Ministry & Mission

1

ACCOUNTABILITY
The Fear of the Lord

The fear of the LORD is the beginning of wisdom,

and knowledge of the Holy One is insight.

For by me your days will be multiplied,

and years will be added to your life.

If you are wise, you are wise for yourself;

if you scoff, you alone will bear it.

PROVERBS 9:10-12

---

*T**hese verses in the book of Proverbs summarize a lengthy dis-* course on the nature, character and value of wisdom. In the first nine chapters of Proverbs; wisdom is personified and identified with God even in the acts of creation. Wisdom cries out, she utters her voice, she calls and she warns, she teaches and she leads, she invites all who will embrace her to receive life and grace and peace. So these words from the voice of wisdom are brought to conclusion with a statement about beginnings, namely that the fear of the Lord is where wisdom begins.

What is the fear of the Lord? Fear is a feeling of dread, a sensation of awe that overtakes us when we encounter something strange or overwhelming. Real fear stops us dead in our tracks. It overtakes our mind, our emotions and our physical body as adrenaline flows to prepare us for fight or flight. Fear imposes a sense of urgency on us, forcing us to decide how we will respond and what we must do in the face of danger. An unexpected encounter of the dead can be a source of overwhelming dread. In fact, the fear of the dead seems very similar to the fear of God, because the specter of death can be for the living a rude and painful confrontation with ultimate reality. Death sends a powerful, immutable message that there is a God, and that it is fully within God's power to give life and to take it. The fact that we give respect and honor to the dead in our funeral rituals and practices shows that we need a structure for overcoming the reaction to death that comes most naturally—to run away in fear and horror.

The fear of the Lord does not always bear the extreme emotions and reactions that can occur when we encounter death, but it does signify a reverent submission to the will of God motivated by an urgent sense of accountability before the throne of God's power. The fear of the Lord is a deep consciousness of the presence of God everywhere and in everything, the conviction that God is always watching, that God sees and knows our every action and thought. And the fear of the Lord need not be a negative and debilitating experience that leaves us with our knees knocking and our hair standing on end. Rather, it is the awe and reverence with which we can come boldly into God's presence because we are confident of God's care and compassion for us. Yet the fear of the Lord imposes on us the imperative to heed God's voice and to follow God's direction, fully conscious of the potential consequences of disobedience.

So the fear of the Lord is the beginning of wisdom. Wisdom has been defined as the art of being successful. Wisdom is not just what you know, it is what you do with what you know, how you apply the information you have accumulated, how you use your ability to understand. And the book of Proverbs teaches that the single most important thing for us to understand is that God is holy, and that God's holiness has clear and practical consequences for how we conduct our lives.

It is my belief that the real purpose of education is to teach us how to think critically, how to make decisions and how to solve problems. Higher education in the fear of God should not mean learning how to be so narrow and dogmatic and doctrinally correct

that we never entertain a new thought or idea, then claim that this
is how God intended for us to use our minds—by closing them!
Rather, we should raise critical questions in the fear of God, absorb
critical content in the fear of God, devise solutions to tough problems in the fear of God. The fear of God does not make us cowards;
it gives us courage to raise questions and seek understanding as God
gives us light.

[handwritten margin note: end goal of fear of the Lord/ solving problems w/ wisdom]

The fear of the Lord is the beginning of wisdom because it gives
us a good reason for choosing what is right and provides a clear
rationale for repentance when we are wrong. Many people don't care
about making right choices because they don't give a thought to who
God is and what is God's will. But God-fearing people choose the
good because we know we are accountable to God.

[handwritten: I DO GOOD BECAUSE I AM ACCOUNTABLE TO GOD.]

Wisdom and Success

If the fear of the Lord is the *beginning* of wisdom, then what is the
end of wisdom? What is its outcome? The end of wisdom is success,
not measured in the materialistic terms that our society would
dictate to us, but success in the sense of becoming, achieving and
producing all that God has ordained for us as receptacles and
channels of wisdom. When we make right choices, we open the door
for God to do constructive and productive things with our lives. The
book of Proverbs promises that the rewards of wisdom include
longevity—that our days will be multiplied and the years of our lives
increased. The end of wisdom is longevity, productivity and fruitful-
ness—in other words, long life with purpose.

[handwritten margin notes: OUTCOME; LONG LIFE w/ PURPOSE]

When we fear God, wisdom will show us how to make the right
choices and best decisions. In the Scriptures Wisdom is a divine
feminine personality who will take us by the hand and lead us in the
right paths. She will shine a light for our journey when everyone
else around us seems to be stumbling in the dark. She will guide us
to the right answers to life's toughest questions. This is the same
Spirit of which the prophet Isaiah spoke when he said:

A shoot shall come out from the stump of Jesse,
 and a branch shall grow out of his roots.

The spirit of the LORD shall rest on him,
>   the spirit of wisdom and understanding,
>   the spirit of counsel and might,
>   the spirit of knowledge and the fear of the LORD. (Is 11:1-2)

Educated men and women who are responsible Christians should know better than to let our learning, ability and skills be coopted for the service of evil. If we fear the Lord and acknowledge God's authority in every aspect of our work, we can embrace wisdom as a divine guide to success. We can choose careers that will position us to do good, and to help others do good things. As teachers, we can teach good and useful things. As scientists, we can do research that will help to improve people's lives. As computer specialists, we can manage information systems for the good of people. As accountants, we can promote good stewardship of financial resources. As journalists, we can write things that inform and uplift our readers. As musicians, we can put together good sounds and rhythms to help people celebrate God's presence. As public administrators, we can bring ethics and insight to government. Whatever our field of specialization may be, we can choose careers that enable us to do good things for and with people and avoid positions that require us to bring evil or harm to others. For those of us who believe, who are accountable for our gifts, who are linked to others in the love of God, success means discerning the will of God in our decisions and delighting ourselves as God's purpose finds fulfillment in our lives. But the only access any of us has to real success is by the path of God-fearing wisdom.

Empowered by Wisdom

The declaration that the fear of the Lord is the beginning of wisdom illuminates for us three emergent themes with special significance in the life of the church today: stewardship, spirituality and servanthood. Each of these aspects of the Christian life begins with reverence for God, and each is the consequence of the habitual exercise of wisdom.

Stewardship is accountability for the gifts, goods and grace God has given us. Apart from a commitment to stewardship, a college education can become a ticket to the prideful and irresponsible pursuit of pleasure. This is the reason some preachers call the seminary the "cemetery": seminary graduates do not always exercise good stewardship of their education in the service of Christ. Instead, too many seminary graduates use their education as a credential authorizing them to play self-indulgent games with God's church.

Spirituality is the cultivation of a relationship of absolute trust and dependence on God. It is much more than emotion or worship style or the accumulation and display of spiritual gifts. Spirituality means walking with God in the path of wisdom. Apart from a commitment to spirituality, then, a college education can lead us into a totally secular lifestyle and value system that deny the reality of God and the truth of the Scriptures.

Servanthood is the inescapable outcome of a life that is motivated by the fear of God and driven by the love of wisdom. Jesus equated servanthood with greatness, and by his example demonstrated to us that servanthood is the only means by which God's purpose can be accomplished in the world. Without a commitment to servanthood, a college education can create a false sense of prestige and honor that deceives us into thinking that we are too smart and too sophisticated to be bothered with the type of people who would benefit the most from our knowledge. That is a major problem in our society today: too many people view education as granting them the privilege of being served rather than the privilege of serving. If God has given me intellectual gifts and spiritual insight, and I am properly centered in God's creative purpose, then I cannot help but to be a servant and a resource to God's people, and I can count on finding opportunities to help others, whatever my line of work.

For the man or woman who fears God, education becomes empowerment to serve human needs. If we devote ourselves to the cultivation of wisdom, the world will benefit more from our perspective than from our specific skills and brainpower. For our age is marked by a flood of information but also by a famine of wisdom. The fear of the Lord gives us a reason to do what is right, and the world needs to know our reasons for doing what is right and for being accountable. Although the book of Proverbs seems to be addressed to the individual, it bears a strong undercurrent of connectedness to justice and righteousness for the oppressed in the fear of the Lord. This perspective begs for fresh and vigorous expression in our time.

2

COMPASSION
The Kingdom Mandate

Then they also will answer, "Lord, when was it that we

saw you hungry or thirsty or a stranger or naked

or sick or in prison, and did not take care of you?"

Then he will answer them, "Truly I tell you, just as you

did not do it to one of the least of these, you

did not do it to me."

MATTHEW 25:44-45

*T*he twenty-fifth chapter of Matthew's Gospel presents three parables concerning the kingdom of God. In the first thirteen verses of the chapter there is the parable of the ten virgins, which Jesus uses to demonstrate the necessity of preparing for the kingdom by acquiring the wisdom and power of the Holy Spirit, symbolized by the oil in the virgins' lamps. In verses 14-30 there is the parable of the talents, which Jesus uses to illustrate stewardship in the kingdom—that is, prudent investment of the material wealth God has entrusted to God's servants. The remaining sixteen verses of the chapter present the parable of the sheep and the goats, which Jesus uses to explain the kingdom mandate of ministry, which is to serve human needs without respect of persons.

These three parables bear several similarities. In each one the protagonists must reap the consequences of choices they have made. These consequences take the form of rewards and punishments. The wise virgins are rewarded by being allowed to enter the banquet hall when the bridegroom comes; the foolish virgins are punished by being sent away with the words "I do not know you." The good and faithful servants in the second parable are rewarded with increased authority and joy; the wicked and slothful servant is punished by being cast out into outer darkness. In the third case the obedient sheep are rewarded with the inheritance of eternal life, while the disobedient goats are punished with the command to depart into everlasting fire.

The greatest reward is reserved for those who have a track record: not just good words and intentions, but a track record of responding to human suffering without respect of persons, because they respect and honor the image of God in all human beings. The worst punishment seems to be reserved for those who disregard human suffering and in so doing reject Christ, who came into the world as a suffering servant.

The kingdom prepared from the foundation of the world is a realm where all are filled and fed and free. Distinctions based on race, sex, nationality, age and marital status mean nothing there. One is qualified to enter that kingdom by exercising good stewardship of life itself, by ministering life out of the abundance one receives as a divine trust from God. Eternal life is the reward for those who cherish life. Those who feed the hungry, give drink to the thirsty, take in the stranger, clothe the naked and visit the sick and incarcerated become identified with the inbreaking of God's kingdom in the world and move with God in the realm of human affairs. To disobey this mandate is to deny allegiance to the kingdom and the King.

We participate in God's kingdom by caring about what happens to people and doing something about it. The critical factor is doing good without respect of persons. The "goats" would have fed the hungry, cared for the sick and visited the prisoners had they known it was the Lord who was on the receiving end. In other words, they would have shown compassion for one claimed as their own, but not for just anybody. The "sheep" did not care whom they were serving; they showed compassion without prejudice and without discrimination.

Holistic Ministry
The kingdom mandate is a mandate to do holistic ministry in the name of Christ. It has both individual and collective dimensions. Each individual has opportunities to respond to others in need. Each local congregation has opportunities to respond to the needs of its community. And each nation has opportunities to respond to the needs of its own citizens and of other nations, especially in times of disaster or famine. It is no easy thing to carry out this kingdom mandate, because the poor and hungry and homeless and sick and imprisoned remind us of what we would be but for the grace of God.

Ministry is service that meets needs. This is not a gospel of convenience, but one of sacrifice. Nor is it a gospel of prosperity; you don't serve in order to prosper, you prosper as you serve. Many Christian leaders in America are cutting and pasting the gospel to make it fit in with the worst of our social values and political ideologies, in a mass appeal to greed and selfishness. They pervert the words of Jesus to say, "Seek all these material things first, and the kingdom shall be added unto you."

It can be painful, costly and frustrating to minister to "the least of these." Sometimes poor people are ungrateful and resentful when others try to help. Sometimes they try to make those who reach out to them feel guilty for not being poor themselves. But we must feed the poor. Sometimes it is inconvenient to visit the sick, and the sights and smells of the hospital can be sickening to those who visit. But we must visit the sick.

Some people have special gifts of compassion, but all Christians are subject to the mandate to minister as we have opportunity and ability. When we fulfill the kingdom mandate by serving human needs, we become God's answer to the prayers of the poor, we become God's answer to the prayers of the sick and the incarcerated. How often do we stand in the comfort of our sanctuaries to pray, "Lord, remember the sick and shut-in. Lord, be with the hungry and the homeless. Lord, visit the hospitals and the prisons"? Does it ever occur to us that it is not God who needs to remember, because God already knows the needs? It is not God who needs to go, because God is already there, waiting for *us* to come and to visit and to minister. How else do we suppose that God can answer prayer, and honor the Word, and send forth the gospel, except by moving the hearts of people to do the work of ministry?

Whenever we feed the hungry, take in the homeless, visit the hospitals and nursing homes and prisons, we show God's promise to be true. We make good on the good news in the eyes of the dispossessed when we minister to them in the name of the Lord, because our ministry is God loving people through us—God feeds the poor in our kitchens, God comforts the lonely in our embrace, God heals the sick when we lay our hands on them, God consoles the prisoner with our words. This is the mandate of the kingdom, that the people of God cooperate with God by doing God's will. When we pray, "Thy kingdom come, Thy will be done on earth as it is in heaven," as Jesus taught us to pray, our words are empty unless we also commit ourselves to preach and practice a gospel that makes God's kingdom come alive on earth. For the kingdom of God is *within you!*

An important question for Christians is this: With whom do we most readily identify in the world, with the "haves" or with the "have-nots"? Do we identify with power and prosperity and privilege? So do the goats in the parable. Or do we, like the sheep, identify with the poor and the powerless who have been pushed to the margins of church and society?

Notice that it is the nations, not individuals, that are divided as sheep and goats. Thus, the measure of the morality of a nation is how it treats its most vulnerable members.

The Example of Jesus

This parable is spoken by Jesus with a full view of reality. Indeed, Jesus came into this world naked and hungry and crying, which is the same way that you and I and everybody else are born into the world. Jesus came in the most helpless form imaginable, as a baby born to an unwed mother. He laid down all his heavenly glory and power to come into the world as a member of an oppressed minority group, as a little stranger who didn't even have a decent place to be born. Jesus was not born in a palace, he was born in a shelter for animals.

Ever since that time people have tried to put him beside themselves on worldly thrones, in lavish mansions, in grand cathedrals, in the corridors of political power, corporate clout and military might. But Jesus did not come to us that way. He identified with the poor and the dispossessed, and he preached that the disinherited of this world would be first in line to receive the inheritance of the kingdom.

God has entrusted to us wisdom and material resources and life—three ingredients represented by the three parables in Matthew 25—and Jesus has shown us, by his own example, what to do with these things. He taught us to have compassion on the poor because he was poor. He taught us to feed and minister to the hungry because he fed and ministered to the hungry.

If we want to be identified with Christ, then we must have a Christlike attitude toward the poor. For the promise of eternal life is given to those wise and good and faithful and profitable and obedient servants who have exercised good stewardship over what God has entrusted to them by teaching and feeding and lending a helping hand to those who suffer the consequences of poverty and ignorance and disease and despair. When we tolerate or ignore human suffering, we show our identity with the devil and his angels, who delight in human suffering. In so doing we claim a stake in the devil's inheritance, which in the parable is eternal punishment. But when we respond to human suffering and human need, we show ourselves to be identified with Christ. We become eligible to receive our inheritance as heirs of the kingdom, because we have been faithful to the mandate of the kingdom by making the Lord's trust available to do the Lord's work.

Investing in Life

We must invest our lives in life, make life our priority—the abundant, joyful life, in defiance of despair and death. For God is glorified in the compassionate relief of suffering, in our loving response to those who suffer. And God is mocked when people who say they love God refuse to love others and will not respond to anyone's suffering but their own.

The path to eternal life begins with the confession of Jesus Christ as Lord, a public commitment to salvation and holiness. We know that salvation does not consist in works alone, yet it is more than just calling Jesus "Lord." In the parable, even the goats called Jesus "Lord," but in the end they were lost. In the Bible *salvation* has at least two meanings: rescue and wholeness. Salvation means that Jesus rescued us so we can help to rescue others; salvation means also that Jesus has made us whole so that we can minister wholeness to others. And what is holiness, but a commitment to live out socially what we confess spiritually?

Although the path to eternal life begins with salvation and holiness, it leads us beyond our doctrines and disciplines into the realm of compassionate ministry. It takes us along the road of social justice and political empowerment, as we not only respond to immediate physical needs but also address the root causes that divide the "haves" from the "have-nots," forces like sexism and racism and economic injustice. Respect of persons is sin—and you don't have to be black or female or poor to know that.

The Least of These

The path to eternal life orients us to the future. In particular, it challenges us to give priority to meeting the needs of children, children who struggle to grow up in a world that routinely exploits and abuses them, that treats them as unwelcome intruders even before they can be born. Children make up the vast majority of the poor, both in the United States and around the world. Children are the "least" of the "least of these." The forces of sexism, racism, economic exploitation and other social sins produce their most damaging effects on the welfare and the future of poor children.

The path to eternal life ends with our ability to give an account at that final inquiry known as the judgment, when the Lamb slain from the foundation of the world, the one who keeps the book of life, shall say,

> Come, you that are blessed by my Father, inherit the kingdom prepared for you from the foundation of the world; for I was hungry and you gave me food, I was thirsty and you gave me something to drink, I was a stranger and you welcomed me, I was naked and you gave me clothing, I was sick and you took care of me, I was in prison and you visited me. (Mt 25:34-36)

The spirit and the message of this parable are reflected in the words of the old Negro spiritual:

> Sweet little Jesus boy, born in a manger,
> Sweet little Holy Child,
> We didn't know who you was,
> We didn't know it was you.

Because the poor, ignorant African-American slaves identified with Jesus and knew what it was like to be mistreated, they understood the kingdom mandate, to receive one another as they would receive Jesus himself. How much more should we today, with all of our freedoms and affluence and education, be required to understand and respond to the call to compassion!

The promise of eternal life is given to those who give the kingdom mandate priority in earthly life. The parable urges us to discern the face of Christ in the faces of human suffering. None of us can feed every hungry person, or give clothes to all the needy, or provide a home for all the homeless, or minister healing to all the sick, or give justice to all who are imprisoned. The Lord has not called us to eliminate poverty or sickness or injustice, but we are called to be responsive to their effects in people's lives. Jesus said, "You always have the poor with you" (Mt 26:11)—*always* as an opportunity for ministry, *always* as a test of our fitness for God's kingdom.

Our response to human need is the real test of our salvation and our holiness. For if we have been rescued and made whole ourselves, and if we treat others in light of our own testimony, then our holiness will be manifest in our compassion for others. And once we set our sights on fulfilling the kingdom mandate, we can be assured that

God will send us everything we need to get the job done.

So many of our church problems and controversies and our deficits in money and motivation derive from the fact that we have invested our collective lives and energies in the wrong pursuits. Sometimes we squander our material and human resources on matters that have nothing to do with the kingdom of God or the gospel of Christ.

A ministry that employs God's resources to meet human needs is never a dry and dead work, but instead is exciting and exhilarating evidence that the kingdom is at hand. It is time for Christians everywhere to reconsider this kingdom mandate to serve the needs of the present age as both recipients and reciprocators of God's promise. The absolute prerequisite of the promise of life is to honor life in the here and now with compassion. For we cannot embrace God's promise of life in eternity without respecting God's gift of life in the "least of these."

3

EMPATHY
The Golden Rule

In everything do to others as you would

have them do to you;

for this is the law and the prophets.

MATTHEW 7:12

*M*atthew's rendition of the saying of Jesus that has been called the Golden Rule has stood the test of time as a universal ethical principle. The Golden Rule has many variations and forms; indeed, every religion in the world appears to have some version of the Golden Rule in its ethical teaching. Jesus offers the Golden Rule as a summary of the law and the prophets. He was not initiating a new teaching or a radical departure from the past; instead he was restating what he knew from the teachings of the Hebrew Scriptures.

While the Golden Rule may not be unique to the teaching of Jesus or the practice of Christianity, the context in which Jesus presents this teaching is special. In Matthew's text the Golden Rule is connected with the teachings on prayer given in the preceding verses.

Prayer and Ethics
In light of the commandment to pray, the Golden Rule guides us toward a grateful response to the goodness of God. When we ask,

God answers. When we seek, God reveals. When we knock, God opens. "For everyone who asks receives, and everyone who searches finds, and for everyone who knocks, the door will be opened" (Mt 7:8). The theological basis of prayer is faith in the goodness of God. Certainly there would be no point in praying if we didn't believe that God is good. Why ask, unless we believe a good God will answer? Why seek, unless we believe a good God will enable us to find what we are looking for? Why knock, unless we believe a good God is going to open the door and invite us to enter?

Prayer is God doing good things for us at our request, and the only appropriate ethical response we can make to God's goodness to us is to do good to others. When we follow the Golden Rule, we are saying thanks to God for answering our requests, for revealing the answers we seek, for opening opportunities that were closed to us.

Matthew's juxtaposition of the Golden Rule and the teaching on prayer suggests that God is holding us accountable for all the prayers that have been answered on our behalf and for all the good things that have happened to us. Sooner or later we will have the opportunity to give a kind answer to someone who is asking us for something, to show the way to someone who is seeking, to open a door for someone who feels locked out. In other words, when we practice the Golden Rule in response to the goodness of God, we become instruments for God to use in answering the prayers of others.

An old folk expression in the African-American community says, "What goes around, comes around." When God is good to me, I want to be good to others. And when I am good to others, God returns good to me. While we can be assured that God is good to us apart from our good works, it especially pleases God when we are good to others.

Releasing God's Power

The Golden Rule guides us toward a practical witness of God's love. Jesus brings his teaching on prayer down to a very practical level, using the illustration of a father's generous response to the requests of his own son. It is no extraordinary exercise of morality for parents to do good things for their own children. Anyone can be expected to be generous to his or her own children, because it is the responsibility of parents to take care of their children's needs. Under normal circumstances, any parents will do anything to provide for their children, whether they are Christian or not. What Jesus establishes here is the notion that God is to us as a divine parent, one who can be trusted absolutely, because God is absolutely good and absolutely capable.

Our earthly parents may do the best they can, but their goodness and generosity are necessarily limited. Jesus suggests that even the evil ones among us know how to give good gifts to our children. So by comparison to earthly parents, how much more is a good God going to give good things to those who ask based on the claims of a parent-child relationship!

Therefore, Jesus says, do good to others, not only to your own children, but to everyone you can, as a witness to the loving relationship you have with God as parent. Just about anybody will do good to those who do good to them, but when you stretch beyond that to do good to those who are your enemies, your actions become a witness to the unique moral depth and quality of God's love. God can love our enemies through us, with the practical consequence that these enemies may feel convicted to change their hostile behavior. When we practice the Golden Rule, we show the world whose children we are, who has ultimate authority in our lives, who has been good to us.

The Golden Rule is a way of life that releases God's power to overcome evil with good. In most English translations of Matthew's formulation of the Golden Rule the initiative comes first, then the action follows. The most popular rendering of the Golden Rule is "Do unto others as you would have them do unto you." But a more accurate statement of this teaching is "All things you want done to you, do to others."

So to follow the Golden Rule as a way of life, we must acquire the habit of thinking, *How would I want to be treated in this situation?* and then letting this reflection guide us in deciding how to treat others. In other words, we must ask ourselves, *What would I want someone to do for me if I were in their shoes?*

When we implement the Golden Rule in this manner, God's authority can be released in our empathy. Empathy is feeling for the other person. And human empathy can become a channel of divine authority when we take the moral initiatives directed by the Golden Rule. It can be seen as a principle of positive interdependence that commences when one person takes the initiative to reflect first on others' needs. Instead of beginning with my reaction to what someone has done to me, I begin with reflection on how I would want to be treated in light of my understanding of who God is and the good things God has done in my life.

An Empowering Principle for the Oppressed

It helps to keep in mind that Jesus was giving this teaching to a crowd of oppressed people, people whom the Romans had pushed and shoved around at will, forcefully and brutally. Jesus was telling them that they did not have to spend their entire existence fretting over what other people had done to them and were conspiring to do to keep them in a downtrodden condition. Whoever we are and whatever our station in life, the Golden Rule gives us authority to take the moral initiative to do good in the world, to give priority to the plans and expectations that God has placed before us, to let God's goodness be produced and multiplied in us, even to the benefit of our enemies and oppressors.

The problem is that so many people don't know how to think of themselves in a positive way and don't really know what it is to be loved and valued and respected. Our society calls this condition "lack of self-esteem," and we tend to blame every social problem, every teen pregnancy, every broken family, every case of drug or alcohol addiction, every crime, every murder, every rape on lack of self-esteem. The Golden Rule offers us a way out of the trap of low self-esteem by encouraging us to begin by thinking of who God is and how God responds to our needs, answers our prayers and treats us better than even the most loving mother or father. It urges us to think about who we are, made in God's image, part of a creation that God declared to be good. We must think about how God intended for us to be happy and blessed and joyful and loved and fulfilled. Then we can make this idea the basis of our desire for others, so that we can treat them as we would want God to treat us, love them as we would want to be loved, help them as we would want to be helped, encourage them as we would want to be encouraged.

Moreover, we must realize that the Golden Rule does not hold us responsible for others' response; our sole responsibility is to take the initiative to do good. Then we can avoid the folly of rendering evil for evil as a way of life.

Much suffering is caused when the Golden Rule is replaced by the iron rule of revenge in people's hearts and minds. Even when dealing with systemic, organized, oppressive, ideological evil that singles out persons and communities for destruction based on their race or sex or some other human characteristic, Christian believers cannot afford to allow the rule of revenge to transform us into the very same kind of monster we are trying to defeat. The tables have a way of turning on those who react rather than initiate in the realm of moral decision-making. We can adopt the Golden Rule with the confidence that God will make a way to get evil out of our way.

The Golden Rule is "golden" because it works for anyone and everyone. It is so simple that even a small child can learn to live by it, because this rule meets each one on his or her own level. If in any situation we don't know what to do, this principle is always the right thing to do, because it is a practical and logical application of the law of love.

The Golden Rule is the fulfillment of the Law and the Prophets, which represent both the commandments of God and the critical application of these commandments in situations of injustice. If we follow all the Bible's teachings on salvation and spirituality and suffering and sacrifice but neglect to honor the Golden Rule in our day-to-day lives, then our Christian testimony will be sadly lacking in credibility.

The Golden Rule is an empowering principle that can convey

moral and spiritual authority in any situation we face. By this teaching Jesus invites every believer to engage in the self-critical application of godly morality in human relationships, and especially to let empathy govern our relationships with persons or groups who differ from us in race, sex or class.

PART II
THE PROPHETIC
MINISTRY OF WOMEN

4

MOTHERHOOD & REDEMPTION

Then Simeon blessed them and said to [Jesus'] mother Mary,

"This child is destined for the falling and the rising

of many in Israel, and to be a sign that will be opposed

so that the inner thoughts of many will be revealed—

and a sword will pierce your own soul too."

LUKE 2:34-35

---

*I*n the first chapter of the book of Genesis, there is an account of how God brought the world into existence. In this story there emerges a very special pattern of speaking and acting. At each stage of the creation narrative, God speaks things into existence, then acts to set those things in place or in motion exactly as they should be. God says, "Let there be light." Then God acts on those words by dividing the light from the darkness. God says, "Let there be a sky." Then God divides the waters below from the waters that rain down from the heavens. Next God separates the water from the dry land and calls the earth to bring forth vegetation. God calls for lights to mark time and seasons and signs, and follows these words with the creation of the sun, moon and stars. The waters bring forth life, the earth brings forth life, and all these species are commanded to be fruitful and multiply.

The pattern shifts, however, as the creation comes to its culmination. God speaks the word for man and woman to come into being: "Let us [the word for God used in the Hebrew is the feminine plural *Elohim*] make humankind in our image." God then directs them to have dominion not over each other, but over the fish, birds and animals. Thus God creates them as male and female in God's own image. God blesses them by telling them to reproduce themselves. If God had followed the pattern of the previous acts of creation, the text would read, "And God said, 'Let there be humankind,' and there was humankind." But the narrative shows that when God creates humankind, God creates them as family, male and female together, with a commandment to bring forth children. In effect, instead of "Let there be man," God says, "Let there be family."

Woman: Divinely Appointed Help

The second chapter of Genesis provides a somewhat different version of how human beings were created. God forms the man from the dust and breathes life into his nostrils. Then God forms the animals and birds and authorizes the man Adam to give them names. The first thing God attends to after creating the man and the world of living things in which he is to work is to create someone to help him. God says, "It is not good that the man should be alone. I will make him a help that fits him" (see Gen 2:18).

The word translated in most English versions of the text as "help" does not mean a subordinate or sidekick. Rather, it signifies the help that comes to us from God. The same word is found in Exodus 18:4, where Moses names his son "Eliezer (for he said, 'The God of my father was my help, and delivered me from the sword of Pharaoh')." The psalmist uses the same word when declaring,

I lift up my eyes to the hills—
from where will my help come?
My help comes from the LORD,
who made heaven and earth. (Ps 121:1-2)

The woman God makes for the man, then, is not just a companion or a crutch. She is to be his divinely appointed help. Perhaps the man could have found a faithful companion or helper among the animals—a cat or dog to keep him company, a horse to ride, a cow to provide milk—but no animal could meet his need for help in the way the woman could.

When God brings the woman to the man, having fashioned her from the man's rib—or to be more exact, the man's side—two significant statements are made in the text with respect to relations between the sexes: (1) the man states that the woman is "bone of my bones and flesh of my flesh" (Gen 2:23)—that is, of the same species, unlike the other creatures; and (2) the two become "one flesh" (v. 24)—that is, marriage is instituted based on the principle of separation and unity, as the man leaves his family of origin to unite with his wife. The further comment that they both were "naked" and "not ashamed" (v. 25) illustrates the nature and depth of their intimacy.

The Death of Innocence

The third chapter of Genesis is the story of how the peaceful paradise of this man and woman is interrupted by deception, disobedience and death. The story seeks to explain the moral and spiritual predicament of humankind. The serpent deceives the woman by convincing her to do the very thing God has forbidden: to eat fruit from the tree of the knowledge of good and evil.

Deception is the basic character of evil. When evil is at work, it becomes increasingly difficult to tell what is true and what is false, or to discern right from wrong. Once the woman has been deceived, she easily disobeys because she is overtaken with delight and desire for the very thing she had been told not to touch. She shares the forbidden fruit with the man, and together they disobey God.

The initial indication of the death of innocence is the statement "Then the eyes of both were opened," and the first thing they see is their nakedness. Presumably, before they sinned they saw only the goodness and beauty of their bodies. After they sin, their nakedness produces feelings of shame and vulnerability and increases their awareness of the risks of hurt and humiliation. Sin then initiates them into a pattern of alienating behaviors—hiding, blaming, denying, making excuses.

God's manner of response to this situation foreshadows the sacrificial dimension of redemption: God shows mercy by clothing them with garments of skins, presumably procured by the sacrifice of live animals.

The death of innocence and intimacy necessitates their expulsion from the garden paradise. The words God utters in response to the human predicament invoke both curses and consequences. God does not curse the woman or the man; instead God curses the serpent who deceived them and the soil. But to the man and woman God speaks a word of redemption. *Redemption* literally means buying back; to redeem is to release by making a payment or complying with some other demand—to ransom, to rescue, to deliver.

Redemptive Motherhood

God's remedy for sin relates redemption to motherhood. The woman's offspring will crush the serpent, who is the embodiment of evil. In cursing the serpent, God offers a word of redemption to and through the woman who will become mother.

The three aspects of this redemptive motherhood revealed in the account of God's response to the sinful disobedience of the man and the woman are characteristic of the overall biblical paradigm for prophetic ministry: struggle, suffering and servanthood. The enmity God places between the serpent and the woman is a divinely ordained struggle between the forces of good and evil, life and death. For the mother redemption is a painful labor of love experienced in the process of giving birth—she suffers. The redemptive servanthood of the mother is readily seen in relation to the word to the man, that he must work hard to feed himself and his family because the soil is cursed. A partnership of redemptive servanthood emerges—the mother labors in childbearing while the father labors as breadwinner, both toward the end of serving human needs.

And when his labors are ended, the man will return to the dust from when he came. Thus the cycle of life and death is set in motion. The man names his wife Eve, because she will become "the mother of all living." Death is inescapable, but the woman is named "mother" or "life-bearer," signifying her role in bringing forth new life and new hope. Therefore death is not the last word on the human condition.

The institution of motherhood figures greatly in God's response to the death and despair the man and woman brought upon themselves by their disobedience. Instead of condemning them to die, God gives the man and the woman the opportunity to perpetuate life. Motherhood, then, represents an alternative to the total destruction of human life as God created it. God's antidote for the deception, the disobedience and the death that overwhelm the human condition is the life-bearing role of mother.

The woman who sinned is designated as the mother of all living. The grace of redemption is manifested in the acts of motherhood—the struggle to affirm life in a world plagued by alienation and despair, the suffering of labor and delivery, and the nurture and discipline rendered to children as loving service.

Mary as Mother of a Savior

The plan of redemption finds fulfillment in the motherhood of Mary, an unmarried teenager who conceived and gave birth to Jesus, a son whose name signified that he would save his people from their sins (Mt 1:21). Mary is presented in all four Gospels as an ideal mother in many respects. The redemptive aspects of her role as mother correspond to the three categories discerned in Eve's story: struggle, suffering, and servanthood.

According to Mary's own prophetic utterance, her pregnancy signifies God's readiness to bring justice to the struggle of the oppressed by reversing the fortunes of the rich and the powerful:

He has brought down the powerful from their thrones,
    and lifted up the lowly;
he has filled the hungry with good things,
    and sent the rich away empty. (Lk 1:52-53)

The suffering Mary would experience is foretold by Simeon on the occasion when the infant Jesus was brought to the temple: "This child is destined for the falling and the rising of many in Israel, and to be a sign that will be opposed so that the inner thoughts of many will be revealed—and a sword will pierce your own soul too" (Lk 2:34-35).

Of course Mary's story begins with her assuming the posture of servant of the Lord. When the angel Gabriel announces that she will become a mother, she responds with words reminiscent of the prophet Isaiah: "Here am I, the servant of the Lord; let it be with me according to your word" (Lk 1:38).

Mary's redemptive ministry of motherhood continues as her child grows up and becomes a man. When the twelve-year-old Jesus gets separated from his parents after the Passover and opts to stay behind in Jerusalem to sit among the teachers in the temple without his parents' knowledge or permission, it is Mary who speaks the words of confrontation and rebuke: "Child, why have you treated us like this? Look, your father and I have been searching for you in great anxiety" (Lk 2:48). Then Jesus returns with them to Nazareth, having learned an important lesson in obedience.

The Gospel of John records that the first miracle Jesus performed was to turn water into wine at a wedding in Cana (Jn 2:1-12). Mary began by informing him that the wine had given out, then, disregarding his protest that the problem did not concern him because his hour had not yet come, directed the servants to follow his direction. There was a direct confrontation between mother and son. But with words showing deep sensitivity with respect to the shortage of wine, the embarrassment of the hosts and the power Jesus had, Mary prompted him to "reveal his glory" by performing his first miracle.

It is recorded in Mark's Gospel that as soon as Jesus appointed the twelve "to be with him, and to be sent out to proclaim the message" (Mk 3:14), a crowd gathered to declare his insanity, and the scribes claimed he was demon-possessed. Then his mother and brothers acted to rescue and restrain him.

One of the most difficult aspects of motherhood is knowing when and where and who to let go, discerning how not to stifle the child's development but at the same time how to remain a responsible, sensitive parent. In the role of protector Mary wants to rescue Jesus—from the crowd, from the frantic pace, from his critics and enemies. But Jesus insists that she release him to do the will of God, even if she cannot fully comprehend what he is called to do and become. In this instance Mary and his brothers have pushed Jesus to introduce a new and different notion of kinship based on faith and obedience rather than blood ties. He asks, " 'Who are my mother and my brothers?' And looking at those who sat around him, he said, 'Here are my mother and my brothers! Whoever does the will of God is my brother and sister and mother' " (Mk 3:31-35).

It is at the foot of the cross that we see the final convergence of motherhood and redemption in Mary's experience. There is perhaps no greater grief on earth than a mother's at having to watch her own child suffer and die. At Calvary Mary stands as Jesus' most treasured and faithful disciple, with unique status as his partner in suffering, because she is the only one who has walked the whole road with him, from the manger to the cross. Although Jesus directs one of the male disciples to take Mary into his own home, it is significant that his mother leads the delegation of mourning women who witness the horrifying scene of redemptive suffering. To his heavenly Father Jesus cries out, "My God, my God, why have you forsaken me?"—to his earthly mother his plea is simply, "Woman, behold your son."

The Significance of Motherhood: Promise and Fulfillment

To summarize, Eve and Mary are two of the many mothers in the Bible who played a significant part in God's plan of redemption. Eve represents the "mother of all living," without whom there can be no human race; Mary's name means "bitter," signifying the suffering without which there can be no redemption.

The sin of Eve has been used for centuries to justify the subjugation of women. The virgin mother Mary has been set forth in some quarters to reinforce notions of female inferiority in the face of an ideal of womanhood that must be emulated but can never be attained. Yet when viewed in their respective roles as mothers, both Eve and Mary figure greatly in God's redemptive plan to restore life and hope to fallen humanity, both male and female. In this light their stories should serve to liberate and enlighten modern-day mothers rather than to burden them with guilt and condemnation. Eve's story demonstrates that a mother's mistakes of the past need not negate her ability and intention to be a good parent if God has spoken to her the words of life. Mary shows that even the most virtuous of mothers may encounter difficulty in the effort to discern how to adjust her words and expressions of parental concern in accord with the changing needs and aspirations of her child.

God's promise to Eve is fulfilled in Mary's prophetic partnership with her son Jesus. It is he who strikes the head of the serpent on the cross to effect redemption from the penalty of sin and death; yet the sword that pierces his side also pierces his mother's soul.

The connection between motherhood and redemption has ongoing meaning for Christian mothers of all ages. A mother's struggle for the well-being of her children in a world fraught with deception and death is a redemptive struggle. A mother who has suffered the pains of labor and delivery for the sake of bringing forth life is positioned to gain deeper insight into the sacrificial posture that Jesus assumed in life and in death. A mother who brings a loving spirit of servanthood to the many tasks involved in meeting the needs of children has hope to redeem even the most wayward, willful, underachieving child by the power of God.

The ethics of the gospel finds expression in these two mothers' stories. The principles of accountability, compassion and empathy are at work in the Garden of Eden—the woman is held accountable for her actions, God's compassion is signaled by the intention to let redemption be brought forth by her offspring, and the sacrifice of animals to provide skins of clothing for the man and woman is an act of divine empathy. While carrying the unborn child in her womb, Mary gives prophetic voice to God's justice and mercy, "according to the promise he made to our ancestors, to Abraham and to his descendants forever" (Lk 1:55). Further, she holds her young son accountable for his behavior and nudges him to begin manifesting his miraculous powers once he has become an adult. In time she develops and maintains her own deep sense of accountability to him as parent and as disciple.

The principles of accountability, compassion and empathy are fully enacted at the scene of Jesus' death on the cross. Mary's accountability to her son is manifested by her presence as a faithful follower; Jesus responds to his mother's faithfulness by arranging for her to be cared for by a male disciple. Mary's expressions of empathy and compassion at Calvary had been foretold years before by Simeon. Indeed, she endures the piercing of her own soul in the course of witnessing her son's execution and death. Mary's commitment to gospel ethics comes to final fruition in the upper room, where she joins with the others in praying to be empowered by the Holy Spirit as a witness of Jesus' resurrection throughout the world (Acts 1:8, 14).

5
THE PROPHETIC INITIATIVE

She has done what she could; she has anointed my body

beforehand for its burial. Truly I tell you, wherever

the good news is proclaimed in the whole world, what she

has done will be told in remembrance of her.

MARK 14:8-9

---

*I*n *Mark 14:3-9 we read the story of the woman who anointed Jesus* at Bethany as a prophetic sign of his impending death and burial. She had broken open an expensive alabaster jar containing an even more expensive ointment, nard or spikenard, imported from India. She had poured ointment on Jesus' head as he sat at table in the house of a leper. Once again Jesus is in the company of the marginalized, this time as the guest of a man with a contagious, incurable disease.

The woman's extravagant action attracted the attention and the angry criticism of Jesus' male disciples. They scolded the woman for wasting the ointment on Jesus rather than selling it and donating the proceeds to the poor. They completely missed the symbolic significance of her action, partly because they were in a state of denial concerning Jesus's suffering and death. She had acted out of an understanding beyond their comprehension, she knew what they could not grasp, she did what they never would have thought to do.

Jesus rebuked these men, as he so often had to do. He affirmed that this woman and her actions would be remembered wherever the gospel is preached in the whole world.

She Did What She Could

It is ironic that Christians today know so much about Judas, who accepted money in exchange for betraying Jesus to the authorities, but most of us know very little about the woman disciple whom Jesus predicted would never be forgotten. A few years ago Elisabeth Schüssler Fiorenza set in motion a new wave of biblical scholarship with the publication of *In Memory of Her,* a book that recalls and reconstructs the importance of this woman in the New Testament. This work informs some of the insights offered in this chapter.

Jesus summarizes her important actions with the words "She has done what she could" (Mk 14:8). What did Jesus mean by those words? Clearly he is commending her for her service, and he seems to be saying that she did *all* she could, all that could possibly be done under the circumstances, as he prepared for his execution on the cross. The male disciples argued that the poor *could* have been helped with the money. While they talked about what *could* have been done, the woman just did what needed to be done, without talking, analyzing, criticizing or prognosticating.

The woman did not stand around waiting for someone to grant her permission to do what she did. She demonstrated the courage and initiative of a prophet, one who is willing to speak for God (if not with words, with symbolic actions). She acted in obedience to God, even when nobody else understood or accepted what she was trying to do.

The prophetic initiative requires the ability to discern with precision the right time, the right place and the right thing to do and say. The woman in this story is not guided by imitation or impulsiveness, nor is she hindered by indecisiveness. In the absence of visible role models, mentors and supporters, she takes the prophetic initiative to perform the anointing ritual.

The woman was criticized for her action with words that were insulting even to Jesus. Those present said that to pour the ointment on Jesus was a waste (v. 4). But the intention to help the poor seems to have been just an excuse for discrediting her.

Anyone doing ministry should expect opposition. Sometimes we are opposed by people who are supposed to know what they are doing by virtue of spiritual or ecclesial authority. We may be opposed by the very persons we expect to support us, and it is hard not to become discouraged or disillusioned when this happens.

On the face of it, the male disciples' argument against the woman's extravagant act of discipleship sounds logical and correct. And if anyone should have known about how to do ministry, as Jesus's inner circle of followers, they should have known. But Jesus said they were wrong.

Also, their motives were suspect. I wonder if Judas thought about donating to the poor the money he was paid to set Jesus up for arrest! The fact is that the value of the ointment was more than monetary, and the woman was fully aware of it.

She does not have to answer her opponents—Jesus speaks in her defense. He instructs the disciples to envision a more balanced approach to ministry, where service to the Lord is the proper thing to do when the opportunity is there, and helping the poor is the right thing to do because the opportunity is *always* there.

The opposition is always there too, and ministers must count the cost of doing what God says do when we know other people might not approve. We must learn how to face our opposition armed with words of truth and love. The woman said nothing in her own defense. The challenge is to incorporate Jesus' words into the answers we must give when our acts of ministry are called into question. Perhaps we can learn to respond as Jesus did whenever our opponents try to diminish the importance of our ministries by reducing everything we do to the measure of dollars and cents.

Our best acts of ministry can seem so incomplete and inadequate sometimes, in the face of all that needs to be done and in view of all the power and resources God has made available to us to meet human needs. The needs are indeed greater than our ability to respond, but God's power is much greater still, so we must try. While our ministries are imperfect, there remains no excuse for incompetence and ineffectiveness.

Anointing and Authority

This woman did her best. She went as far as she could go. She held nothing back. Yet she acted under divine authority. Who had revealed to her that Jesus was the Christ, the Anointed One now ready to be anointed for burial? How was she able to foresee his death and burial? Why did she expend the precious imported ointment and its costly container for a merely symbolic act? She did all these things because she was able to envision the challenge of acting on the basis of revelation. It is God who authorized her to act, and Jesus confirmed that divine authorization. God was signifying something through her and in her work. Similarly today, women who minister without licenses or ordination in churches which refuse to authorize women's leadership do not necessarily minister without divine authority.

This woman had to be anointed by God in order to anoint the Son of God. This is not to suggest that her anointing was greater than Jesus' anointing. But just as God had revealed the Christ to Peter at Caesarea Philippi, God revealed the Christ to this woman of Bethany.

The contrast between the two is illuminating here. As soon as Peter made his confession, he rejected Jesus' prediction of His own suffering and death, and then Jesus had to rebuke him with words as harsh as we ever hear Jesus speak. But the woman was more accepting and understanding of this suffering Christ, and her action showed her insight into his sufferings. Jesus spoke no words of rebuke to her, only words of commendation and praise. Indeed, Jesus may have welcomed her action with a great sense of relief and encouragement, that finally somebody understood what he was going through and why!

Jesus promised that whenever the gospel is preached in the future, this unnamed woman disciple should be remembered. Her example speaks pointedly to women who take the initiative to do loving acts for others in the name of Christ, who serve others without allowing cost to be the only concern, who obey God despite opposition and condemnation by others.

The woman of Bethany is a spiritual foremother to women in ministry today, and deserves to be claimed as such. Women in ministry need to take the prophetic initiative, in memory of a woman who served Christ in ways that men did not understand. Women in ministry must face all opponents, in memory of a woman who let Jesus' words become her abiding assurance and her first line of defense. Finally, women in ministry must act with divine authority, in memory of a woman who was anointed to perform the greatest act of anointing in all the history of the world. And when we preach the gospel, whenever we proclaim the good news, let us do it in memory of her, to the glory of God, in the service of Christ, by the power of the Spirit.

6

LETTING THE SPIRIT LEAD
*The Prophetic Witness
of Women
in the Upper Room*

All these were constantly devoting themselves to

prayer, together with certain women, including Mary

the mother of Jesus, as well as his brothers.

ACTS 1:14

*T*he book of Acts opens with an account of Jesus' parting words and his ascension into heaven, then describes how his followers learned to let the Holy Spirit lead them in fulfilling the assignment to be his witnesses in Jerusalem and throughout the world.

The actual parting scene took place on the Mount of Olives, about a half-mile outside of the city of Jerusalem, the same site where Jesus had prayed with his disciples prior to his arrest and betrayal. Here on the Mount of Olives we see the apostles responding in two ways to Jesus as he prepared for his final departure from them—they *listened* and they *looked.*

Listening and Looking
They listened to his last words and instructions, even hanging on every word, it seems. But they listened very selectively, listening for just what they wanted to hear. They wanted to hear that Jesus would

return soon to overthrow their Roman oppressors and restore political power to Israel. And perhaps they were listening also for their own names to be called as they were appointed to positions of authority in this restored kingdom.

Jesus responded to their selective listening with an effort to expand their understanding of what God was doing and when. Their thinking was much too narrow for God's plan. Jesus promised that they would receive power to become witnesses—not national rulers in Israel but witnesses to the world, agents of change and heralds of transformation, leading men and women into God's kingdom.

Another way they responded was by looking. When Jesus finished speaking, he was taken up in a dramatic departure, and a cloud took him out of their sight. Afterward they continued to look; they stared, they gazed up toward heaven. Two men in white robes appeared, asking them why they were standing there looking. These messengers assured them that Jesus would one day return in the same manner as he had left.

The disciples looked up in amazement. But the right way to watch for Jesus' return is not to look *up* but to look *in*—to examine ourselves, to position and prepare ourselves to receive holy power so that we can fulfill our calling to be witnesses to the world. For a few moments, maybe even for a few hours, they looked up, but next they began to look inward, and the Scripture tells us that their next step was to gather themselves for prayer, the supreme posture of inner empowerment.

Women in the Upper Room

The apostles listened, they looked, and now they are ready to be led by the Spirit. Jesus is gone—dead, resurrected and ascended; now where are they going to look for leadership? This is where the women come in. Returning to Jerusalem from the outskirts, they gathered in an upper room with other men and women, including the mother and brothers of Jesus, a group of 120 in all.

This upper-room prayer meeting may have marked the beginning of women's numerical dominance in the church. We don't know how many women were present, but we do know that there were at least eleven men, because they are named in the text—the apostles Jesus had chosen as his most intimate followers and friends. We can add to the tally of men Jesus' brothers, as well as Joseph and Matthias, who were in contention to replace Judas by the casting of lots. Thus there are about fifteen men accounted for in the text. What if the remaining 105 persons present at the prayer meeting were all women? That congregation would have been approximately 83 percent female and 17 percent male.

There are black churches in the United States where women make up 90 percent of the membership, and in almost all churches everywhere, regardless of race or nationality, women make up the vast majority of members. Although women are rarely well represented in the leadership of the churches, and sometimes are excluded altogether from pulpits and positions of power, women are perennially present in the pews.

Women must have been present in significant numbers in the upper room, and also when the day of Pentecost arrived, because Peter interpreted the pouring out of the Holy Spirit by quoting the prophecy of Joel declaring that sons *and* daughters would prophesy, and prophesy they did. Later on some key women leaders emerged in the early church—Lydia, a businesswoman; Prisca or Priscilla, a tentmaker and preacher; Phoebe, a minister of great authority; and Junia, named by Paul as an apostle along with her husband Andronicus.

Although Mary the mother of Jesus was not a leader as such, she was important enough in this gathering to merit mention by name. She is the one woman whose name appears throughout the narratives of Jesus' ministry from beginning to end. As a young expectant mother she prophesied concerning the wondrous things God was doing through her yet unborn son. As an older woman she received the blessing of the Holy Spirit after Jesus' ascension into heaven.

We should never have to apologize for the predominance of women in the churches. Our concern should not be that there are too many women but rather that there are too few men. In Acts 1 the men gave priority to recruiting a man to round out the Twelve. The men are named in their capacity as leaders, but what about the male followers? Sometimes our exclusive emphasis on male leadership not only pushes the women aside but also minimizes the role of men who are not leaders. Sometimes we do an effective job of structuring our church organizations so that women can find a job to do and a role to play, but we don't always succeed at helping men in the pews to find their place of ministry. If only men can do ministry and only women can do "missionary work," where does this leave the women who are called to ministry and the men who are called to missions? How are men going to be won to Christ if men are not sent from the churches to evangelize them? What happens when men and women submit to the leadership of the Spirit, in view of the reality that the Spirit does not discriminate on the basis of sex?

Spiritual Leadership
When we let the Spirit lead, some of our ideas and biases get overruled as the Spirit chooses who should exercise gifts and authority in the church. In Acts the women were excluded from apostolic leadership at first, but the Spirit drew them into the forefront of the church's ministry and witness to the world. How? Through the ministry of prayer.

The text indicates that the men and women came together in one accord, with one heart and one mind, as they continued or persevered in prayer. The quality of their corporate prayer ministry was fostered by a posture of pouring out and kneeling down. This is the prayer that changes things, that gets things done, that opens doors, that brings deliverance, that prepares God's people to be led by the Spirit and equips leaders to lead. The best style of leadership is spiritual leadership, by people who can be trusted to lead as they are themselves led. The Spirit leads men and women according to the models of leadership that Jesus promoted—humble servanthood and compassionate shepherding of God's flock.

Today we need more spiritual leaders and followers. The churches are overpopulated with bystanders, spectators and critics—people who never encourage, build up or create. We need leaders who understand the difference between people-politics and spiritual authority. People can put you into positions of political power—they can vote you in and they can vote you out. People can appoint to ministry, but only the Spirit can anoint for ministry. And when we become empowered by God, we become witnesses for Christ. The whole emphasis shifts away from using power structures to exalt individuals and moves instead toward letting the Spirit shape the structures and empower the people to amplify and increase the witness. A simple and reliable test of any structure, polity or organization to be implemented in the life of the church is to ask whether it will enhance or diminish the church's witness for Christ.

The single most important act of the apostles was to let the Spirit lead. And the course of early church history was clearly shaped by praying, prophesying women who looked to Jesus' example even as they hoped for his return. They listened to God for guidance, and not only to men. Their premier leadership strategy was to let the Spirit lead. Their courage and their prayers helped to lay a firm foundation for the church to grow and flourish, a process that can be continued by women and men who are committed to prayer and empowered to be witnesses.

PART III
MINISTRY AT THE MARGINS
Children & Youth

7

PROPHETIC PARENTING

Then Eli perceived that the LORD was calling the boy.

Therefore Eli said to Samuel, "Go, lie down; and

if he calls you, you shall say, 'Speak, LORD, for your

servant is listening.'"

1 SAMUEL 3:8-9

*W*e parents have the premier responsibility to supervise our children in every aspect of their development to full maturity. The laws of the land hold us accountable for meeting their physical needs—we have to feed, shelter, clothe and protect them from harm, or they are taken away from us. Moreover, society requires us to meet their intellectual needs by sending them to school or, as the case may be, teaching them at home, so that they are socialized intellectually to function as literate, informed adults. But whose responsibility is it to ensure our children's spiritual development? Not the government's, for sure, and not the society's either. The spiritual development of our children is a responsibility shared by the church and the home.

Learning to Listen
The Old Testament book of 1 Samuel (chapter 3) tells the story of how a boy no more than twelve years old had his first encounter with

God, at a time when there were precious few words and visions from God. Young Samuel was sleeping in the sanctuary, near the ark of God, when God spoke. At first Samuel thought the voice of God was the voice of Eli, the priest—a mistake that gets made in reverse sometimes today when we think God is speaking, but it is only a human voice speaking very human words to us. It is not until Samuel identifies himself as God's servant that God speaks with a voice and words that Samuel can understand.

There are two persons in this story, but one of the two plays two distinct roles in light of the prophetic word. First there is Samuel, the young prophet, open, learning, wanting to hear from God but not knowing quite how to answer. Second, there is Eli the priest, who allowed sexual abuse and other outrageous behaviors driven by greed and lust to go on in God's temple; and there is Eli the parent, for his two sons Hophni and Phinehas are the ones responsible for profaning the sanctuary of the Lord.

Samuel makes the transition from boyhood to servanthood when he recites the words taught to him by Eli: "Speak, LORD, for your servant is listening" (vv. 9-10). Embedded in this simple imperative are three critical decision points in Samuel's spiritual development—three phases, three rites of passage that enable him to grow into the divinely appointed position of prophet. First he says "Speak, Lord." Speak, I'm ready to receive, I'm open to communicating with you, at the time when you, Lord, choose to speak. With these words Samuel is not just giving God orders, he is giving God an opening. Second, he calls himself "your servant." I am your servant, Lord. I am at your service, at your disposal, waiting for orders from you. I am disciplined and ready to do the work of ministry. Servanthood, more than charisma, intelligence, age or appearance, is the key to hearing a word from God. Third, he says, "I'm listening"; in other words, I want to hear, I intend to obey, I am open to the truth, and I will be faithful to the message.

God Speaks

When finally God speaks, it is not with gentle words of encouragement or affirmation that we might expect to be conveyed to a young prophet receiving his first divine visitation. Instead God speaks a harsh word of rebuke and condemnation directed at Samuel's mentor, Eli:

> Then the LORD said to Samuel, "See, I am about to do something in Israel that will make both ears of anyone who hears of it tingle. On that day I will fulfill against Eli all that I have spoken concerning his house, from beginning to end. For I have told him that I am about to punish his house forever, for the iniquity that he knew, because his sons were blaspheming God, and he did not restrain them. Therefore I swear to the house of Eli that the iniquity of Eli's house shall not be expiated by sacrifice or offering forever." (1 Sam 3:11-14)

At first Samuel is afraid to repeat what God has said. But after Eli insists, even threatening him, he tells the whole thing, every word that God had spoken. It is in the faithful declaration of the whole counsel of God that the initiation of the prophet is complete—God has spoken, and so the prophet speaks.

A Word of Warning

God uses young Samuel to rebuke Eli in his role as priest. It is as if God was saying to Eli, "If you won't listen, I will find someone else who will hear and tell the truth." His two sons had compromised the quality of the sacrifices people brought to the Lord by taking more than their share of the meat before it had been properly cooked. They exploited the people by taking the meat they had brought to sacrifice to the Lord, and they took it from them by force. Then they had sex with the women who served at the temple entrance. Greed and lust were their priority, not worship, not sacrifice, not service.

Eli's descendants today are peculiar beggars, people who see the ministry as a meal ticket, as an opportunity to make easy money, to have an easy living—people who will pursue ministry as a career, not because they are called but because they are themselves so needy and greedy and lazy.

The prophecy the child Samuel brought against Eli was not the first prophetic warning he had received from the Lord; it was mainly a confirmation, a reiteration of a warning God had already given. A man of God had already come to Eli with a long word of rebuke, declaring that Eli and his sons were disqualified from the priesthood, and the price they had to pay for their shameful mismanagement of God's house and the abuse of God's people was death. In addition, God had promised to raise up a faithful priest who would know the heart and mind of God, who would honor God in thought and feeling.

God also rebuked Eli as a parent. God used a child to administer a verbal spanking to the parent. Samuel's mother Hannah had given him to the elderly priest Eli to fulfill a vow she made to the Lord at the same temple where Eli served. She had prayed there and poured out her soul before God because of her infertility. Eli noticed her and gave a compassionate, priestly response to her petition. And when God answered her request and she became a mother, she prayed a prophetic prayer of thanksgiving:

The LORD kills and brings to life;
> he brings down to Sheol and raises up.
The LORD makes poor and makes rich;
> he brings low, he also exalts.
He raises up the poor from the dust;
> he lifts the needy from the ash heap,
to make them sit with princes
> and inherit a seat of honor. (1 Sam 2:6-8)

Hannah's prophetic words are echoed in her son's oracle against Eli, and his sons, who have become God's enemies. But at the time when Hannah speaks these words, she leaves her newly weaned firstborn son Samuel in Eli's care. Why would Eli, who had missed his own calling as parent to his own sons, be trusted as a mentor for Samuel? Maybe this is God's way of saying that parents are deserving of a second chance. If we make mistakes with our own children, it does not necessarily mean that we cannot be of help and encouragement to someone else's child.

Whatever we make of Eli's horrible failure as a parent of two wicked sons on the one hand and his capable mentoring of the young prophet Samuel on the other, it is clear that God held him responsible for the defilement of the temple. But Eli does not deny or reject the word from Samuel. Instead he confirms that God has indeed spoken to him through the child, and receives his rebuke with a spirit of submission: "It is the LORD; let him do what seems good to him" (1 Sam 3:18).

Scripture tells us that as Samuel grew, the Lord was with him and made everything he said come true. His prophetic ministry was so great that his words never "fell to the ground" (3:19). In other words, when Samuel spoke his words always found their target in the hearts and minds of the people. Indeed, every preacher, every modern-day prophet, ought to aspire to Samuel's level of prophetic proficiency and to seek the assurance that every sermon we preach is a message from God to meet the needs of the people, even if our words are words of rebuke.

But even Samuel turned out to be a better prophet than parent. He made his sons judges in Israel, but they "did not follow in his ways, but turned aside after gain; they took bribes and perverted justice" (1 Sam 8:3).

Failed Parenting

How did it happen that Eli's sons did not know the Lord at all, that they were "sons of Belial" (1 Sam 2:12 KJV)—an expression that means they were worthless, reckless, lawless scoundrels? They were the priest's kids, but they did not understand or respect the priestly ministry. Why not? Perhaps because Eli did not take the time to teach them, didn't give them guidance and instruction in the ways of the Lord when they were growing up, as he did for his young charge Samuel.

We encounter a similar reference to Belial (Beliar), which is another name for Satan or the devil, in Paul's prophecy to the troublesome Corinthian church:

> What agreement does Christ have with Beliar? Or what does a believer share with an unbeliever? What agreement has the temple of God with idols? For we are the temple of the living God; as God said,

"I will live in them and walk among them,
    and I will be their God,
    and they shall be my people.
Therefore come out from them,
    and be separate from them, says the Lord,
and touch nothing unclean;
    then I will welcome you,
and I will be your father,
    and you shall be my sons and daughters,
says the Lord Almighty." (2 Cor 6:15-18)

Guiding Our Children

Paul's words to the Corinthians suggest that we should do what we can to help our children understand that they belong to God and that they must choose God for themselves. The highest aim of Christian parenting is to see our children *become* children of God—to help our children learn to treat their bodies as the temple of God, by our example more than by our words alone. Otherwise they may grow up like Hophni and Phinehas, having great contempt for God and the church, defiling the sanctuary with their wickedness, preferring the company of the unrighteous and unbelievers to the fellowship of the people of God, rubbing their own noses in the unclean thing, using their bodies as temples of greed and lust and not as temples of the living God.

We cannot force our children to become Christians, and it may happen that they will rebel against our best efforts to nurture them to faith and belief in Jesus Christ. But still we must try—we must love them and have faith in them, and we must be realistic about the power and attractiveness of the forces of evil that compete with God for their attention and allegiance from the earliest stages.

One of the most important things we can do is to monitor the images and ideas our children are exposed to on television, in books and magazines, and at school. Evidently Hophni and Phinehas had plenty of opportunity when they were growing up to observe sexual misconduct and exploitative practices. And this all happened centuries before cable television, gangsta rap, X-rated movies, pornographic magazines and other modern inventions that seduce and deceive our children by feeding them evil ideas and images.

Eli's major mistake as a parent was that he honored his sons above God. And when he fully realized how wicked they had become, it was too late. He tried to correct them, but they would not listen to him—they disrespected their father as much as they disrespected God (see 1 Sam 2:22-25).

In 1 Samuel 4 we read of the horrible fulfillment of the prophecies against Eli and his sons. The people of Israel are surprised when they are defeated by the Philistines. Hophni and Phinehas, of all people, take the ark of the covenant with them into battle. Israel is defeated again, Hophni and Phinehas are killed, and the ark is captured by the enemy. When Eli receives word that his sons have been killed and the ark has been taken, he falls over backward and breaks his neck. When the bad news is given to Phinehas's pregnant wife, she immediately goes into labor and faces death herself. But before she dies, she names the child Ichabod, meaning "The glory has departed from Israel."

Indeed the glory had departed from Israel—not just because of the power of the Philistines but also because of the failed parenting of Eli and the priestly misconduct of his sons. This was not only a military defeat, but the spiritual devastation and demoralization of an entire people.

Parenting Prophetically

When God speaks to Samuel, the child's prophetic word is a warning to the priest who is the parent of the offending children. How can parents, as religious educators, as pastors and youth workers, avoid making the same mistakes with our own children? We must begin the same way young Samuel was taught to do, by saying, "Speak, Lord, I'm listening."

Eli's sons were spoiled—they were caught up in satisfying themselves with material things taken from other people. They were spoiled because Eli honored his sons, and what they wanted, over and above God and what God willed. And eventually Eli was rendered powerless in his efforts to exercise parental authority over them. Thus we must resist the temptation to become so consumed with materialism that our children have no sense of what it means to make sacrifices. We must resist the tendency to measure every worship experience with the yardstick of convenience and recognize that God has called us to commitment and not to comfort.

Boredom and lack of parental supervision have as much to do with teen sexuality and pregnancy as does low self-esteem. Eli remained unresponsive to his sons's outrageous behavior until it was too late to do anything about it.

The church is at a point where we must decide how much priority in funding, planning and human resources we want to devote to preparing our children for ministry. Do we regard families in our churches as consumers or as producers? The problem is that many of us in the church see our purpose as ministry *to* families, in the sense of feeling compelled to meet everyone's needs, to make everything convenient, to make everybody feel they can have it all. Instead we must give more emphasis to empowering the ministry *of* families, to help each family to find ways of discerning the work God has for that family to do as a unique mission base.

The Christian family is a potential powerhouse of intergenerational ministry and mission, where parents and children learn and work together to do tasks that no one individual can do alone. We are not called into the church as parents and children to be entertained and spoiled; families are called to hear God's Word, seek God's face and do God's work. Parenting becomes prophetic ministry and mission when parents and children discover mutual spiritual empowerment, not just to pray together but also to work and grow together as servants of God.

8

YOUR SONS & DAUGHTERS SHALL PROPHESY

In the last days it will be, God declares, that I will pour

out my Spirit upon all flesh, and your sons

and your daughters shall prophesy.

ACTS 2:17

*B*oth the Old and New Testaments testify of the importance of children in the work of God and the move of the Spirit. Moreover, specific roles and significance are ascribed to children in biblical prophecy, notably as Old Testament prophecies are interpreted in New Testament contexts. One important example of this is found in the second chapter of the book of Acts, when the prophecy of Joel finds fulfillment in the empowering witness of the early church.

The Pentecost event recorded in the second chapter of the book of Acts is recognized by Christians as a mighty outpouring of God's Spirit upon a company of praying men and women in the presence of an international gathering of devout worshipers. The word *Pentecost* refers to the fifty days, or seven weeks, after the Passover when the Jews observed the Feast of Weeks in celebration of the spring

---

An earlier version of this chapter appears under the title "A Children's Pentecost" in *Prophetic Voices: Black Preachers Speak on Behalf of Children*, ed. Allegra S. Hoots (Washington, D.C.: Children's Defense Fund, 1993).

harvest of wheat and the revelation of the law to Moses at Mount Sinai.

People present at this Pentecost included the 120 disciples of Jesus Christ who were praying when the Spirit gave them power to speak with other languages; the global community of Jews living in Jerusalem, representing every nation under heaven, and every race (as we use that word today), Africans, Asians and Europeans who heard the disciples speak God's praises in their own languages; a crowd of spectators who mocked the ecstatic behavior of the believers and accused them of being drunk; and the prophet Peter, who stood and spoke as an interpreter of these happenings in light of the Scriptures.

Peter proclaimed that these people were not drunk at all, especially not so early in the day, but were celebrating the wonderful works of God under the influence not of alcohol but of the Spirit. The scriptural basis for Peter's interpretation and explanation of this event was the prophecy of Joel, where God promises to pour out the Spirit on all flesh, that is, on all kinds of people, and to cause sons and daughters to prophesy, young men to see visions, old men to dream. Even slaves, those men and women who have the greatest poverty and the least power in any society, would receive this outpouring and speak God's word.

An Outpouring upon the Marginalized

The prophecy goes on to say that wonders and signs in heaven and earth would cause men and women to call on the name of the Lord and be saved. Saved from what? Saved from poverty and hunger and shame, those who worship and call upon the name of the Lord in Jerusalem would escape the terrible day of the Lord. Saved for what purpose? Saved for the fresh, new beginning God wanted them to have as an oppressed people, no longer defeated but victorious, no longer scorned and demoralized but empowered to do what was just and right. Among these would be a remnant of survivors whom the Lord called. And God calls in order to position people, far and near, to receive the promise of the Holy Spirit—especially the children.

This is a children's Pentecost. The promise of God, the gift of the Holy Spirit, the good news of Jesus Christ—all are given to us and our children (Acts 2:39). Joel said, "Your sons and your daughters shall prophesy"—yes, opening doors for women to preach and speak prophetically, but just as important, making children the direct beneficiaries of this promise. Children and slaves, the ones most vulnerable, the ones most easily exploited and abused, the ones whose oppressed state is most readily discerned—these are the ones God has chosen to receive the outpouring of the Spirit and to bear the prophetic proclamation.

On the day of Pentecost, Peter preached so powerfully to the people that they were moved in their hearts to respond with a simple question that continues to guide our response to God's word today: "What should we do?" (2:37). Peter's somewhat complex answer to this question is a helpful guide for those of us who would seek a children's Pentecost in our own time. He begins by telling them to repent—to change their minds; be baptized in a public confession of their newfound spiritual identity; be forgiven—rather than denying or covering up, be honest before God about their faults and shortcomings; and receive the gift of the Holy Spirit—not approaching God with doubt or with fear but rather with an openness to the profoundly spiritual ways in which God's power and presence can be mediated to and through people.

Next the Scripture says of Peter that "he testified with many other arguments and exhorted them." It takes many words, and questions, and testimonies, and exhortations to persuade and influence people, young or old, to change their perspective. No one simple solution or formula will work every time. The true challenge is to find the appropriate word, the right question, the credible testimony, the exact exhortation that will encourage others to examine their own predicament in light of God's promise and will assure them that "the promise is for you, for your children, and for all who are far away, everyone whom the Lord our God calls" (Acts 2:39). What a difference it can make if we find words to convince others that it is God who is calling them to something better!

Finally Peter tells the people to "save yourselves from this corrupt generation," words we would do well to repeat to our children. This is a hard saying: though perhaps we can't save them from all the perils and pitfalls plaguing their peers, let us at least try to warn them of the consequences of wrong choices and at the same time steer them toward the doors God is opening for them.

Preparing Children for Pentecost

The implications of this interpretation of Acts and Joel are many for those of us with a concern for the plight of children in today's world. As Christian parents we must believe God's promise and prepare our children to become responsive to God's Spirit—by nurturing them in our faith traditions, by taking them frequently to our places of worship so that they feel at home there, by allowing our own character to be molded and shaped by the Spirit of God so that our children will be motivated to emulate the godly virtues they observe in us. Many of our children feel alienated from God and lose interest in religion at an early age because of the hypocrisy and moral inconsistency of parents and church leaders.

There is a reckless abandon in the worship style of these New Testament "Pentecostals" that reflects the energies and aspirations of youth. The high level of excitement and ecstasy and enthusiasm in their worship caused critics to accuse them of drunkenness. Today drug and alcohol abuse are rampant among young people of all classes and races, sometimes more so in the suburbs than in the inner cities, and inebriation is a state more readily recognized (and more frequently observed) than exhilaration. Has society misled and duped them into thinking that the only way to have a good time is to follow advertisements and other media images that encourage getting high on harmful substances? Is it possible to design worship experiences for our youth that make use of the sounds and rhythms and words they find attractive in order to convey positive messages about God, self and neighbor? Gospel music, for example, which was born and bred in the African-American Pentecostal churches, provides an exciting synthesis of contemporary music with inspirational messages that can be used effectively to reach children and youth in churches, schools and other settings.

While it may not be wise to try to replicate the atmosphere of the rock concert or the hip-hop culture in the church, it wouldn't hurt to loosen up a bit by using music, drama, rap and other elements that reflect our acknowledgment of what appeals to children if we have a serious desire to keep them plugged into what God is doing and saying in our faith communities. Can young people have a good time at church, in an environment that encourages a self-affirming encounter with God as an alternative to the self-destructive escape from reality afforded by drug and alcohol use?

The promise given to Joel as invoked by Peter at Pentecost challenges us as parents and as a society to make our children our number-one priority. Most of the social problems we observe in our cities and schools, evident in the soaring rates of violent crime, premature sexual activity and sexually transmitted diseases among teens, dropping out of school and unemployment can be traced to the breakdown of the family and a massive crisis in parenting. Even the most well-meaning parents are at a loss as to how to deal with their children, and there are precious few places where the "good" or the "bad" parents can go to receive instruction, guidance and support.

Children act out rebellion against parents, and parents act out rejection of their children. Many children, both rich and poor, are growing up in households where they are ignored and neglected when small, then feared and despised as they grow older. These parents tend to give more attention to their own needs, problems and plans than they do to the development of their children. Unfortunately, our society tends to discount the concerns and contributions of children in its allocation of goods and resources. In so many ways we curse our children rather than bless them—then we are shocked when they begin to treat others (including parents) in the same abusive manner with which they have been treated.

If we as a community of parents sincerely believe that God has promised to give divine gifts to our children, to pour out a children's

Pentecost upon them so that they can experience joy and peace and love and power as vehicles of God's truth, then we will shift our priorities to bless our children rather than curse them, empowering them emotionally, intellectually and spiritually to fulfill God's calling on their lives, for their sake and for ours.

9

EMPOWERING THE NEXT GENERATION

But Paul went down, and bending over him took

him in his arms, and said, "Do not be alarmed,

for his life is in him."

ACTS 20:10

*C*hildren and youth are at the center of attention in many of the stories the New Testament tells about the ministry of Jesus and the emergence of the early church. In particular, the book of Acts records several accounts of the involvement of young people in the ministry of the apostles.

Rhoda: Youthful Enthusiasm

In Acts 12:12-17 we read of Rhoda, an exemplar of youthful enthusiasm. Enthusiasm is a characteristic trait of young people, who tend to have a surplus of energy and optimism compared with older people. The problem is that this enthusiasm is not always balanced with the practicality of good common sense. Presumably Rhoda was a part of the prayer meeting that was going on in the house of Mary the mother of John Mark, where the church had gathered to pray for

Peter while he was in prison. As the prayer meeting continued, Peter was miraculously delivered from prison and came knocking at the outer entrance to the house.

Rhoda is a slave, so it is her duty to answer the door. She is overjoyed when she recognizes Peter's voice. But instead of letting him in, she runs back to tell the others that their prayers have been answered. She goes running with *testimony,* leaving *evidence* standing outside the door. Because Rhoda forgets to let Peter in, when she tells the others the good news they refuse to hear her. They say that she is crazy, or that she has seen an angel.

Her testimony was true, but because she left the evidence behind she had a hard time being heard. And being young and female and a slave did not help her credibility at all! The others thought they had every reason not to listen to her. Peter had to keep knocking until someone else let him in, because Rhoda's enthusiasm had overwhelmed her good judgment.

A Slave Girl's Exploitation and Deliverance

Rhoda's story has a humorous side, but there is no humor at all in the story in Acts 16:16-23 of an unnamed slave girl who was exploited and then set free. This young girl was doubly exploited. She was used by the evil spirit that possessed her—a "python" or snake spirit that was worshiped by people who sought its ability to foretell the future. But she was also exploited by greedy men who used her in her oppressed spiritual condition to make money for themselves.

Today there are many persons who see the oppressed spiritual condition of our youth as an opportunity to make money. The producers of cocaine, crack and marijuana, the beer companies, the manufacturers of expensive clothes and shoes—all are examples of businesses that exploit the spiritual and emotional vulnerability of young people to increase their profits. And they especially target the poor, those who can least afford to purchase drugs and designer apparel but who may have the greatest need to buy expensive material things to feel good about themselves. Even toy manufacturers exploit little children and their beleaguered parents by selling cheap plastic toys at high prices, flooding the television with advertisements to convince toddlers and preschoolers that in order to have fun like their peers on the screen they *must* have this toy.

The music industry makes billions of dollars by selling any kind of garbage to youth; what seems necessary to be successful in this business is not musical talent but a seductive beat, profane language, distinctive fashions and bizarre hairstyles. The recording studios thrive on the young consumers's need to feel accepted by their peer group. Although the vast majority of today's rap music is produced by young black males, its verbal assaults on black women feed the racist and misogynist attitudes of many young white males who are drawn to this music. The movie industry also uses contemporary sounds and styles to draw young people into an audiovisual barrage of negative, antisocial messages.

The evil spirit in the young slave girl spoke an admixture of truth and lies, so that this slave of the devil underlined the message of salvation being proclaimed by Paul and his colleagues, the slaves or servants of God! Evil spirits sometimes do tell the truth, but always with a double meaning, so that here it is hard to discern whether Paul and Silas were being taunted or praised. Double-talk is the language of exploitation; only the singular speaking of the truth can set people free.

When Paul commands the evil spirit to come out of the girl, the spiritual and economic exploitation comes to an end. But the double-talk continues. The slaveowners begin to make false accusations against Paul and Silas. They don't say, "Punish them because they took away our meal ticket"; instead they say, "These men are advocating customs that are against Roman law" (see vv. 19-21). Double-talk is designed to say one thing and mean another, all toward the end of accomplishing evil and selfish purposes. As a consequence of this vengeful double-talk, Paul and Silas are publicly stripped, beaten and thrown into jail.

The imprisonment of Paul and Silas under these circumstances sets the stage for a glorious and miraculous deliverance. In jail they keep singing and praying and praising God, keep showing the way of salvation. God sets them free, and the jailer finds salvation. This gospel is a gospel of freedom and not one of oppression and exploitation. Exploitation, on the other hand, is sin. Using other people's spiritual immaturity and disability as an opportunity to make money is always wrong, no matter who is doing it to whom. And it is an especially grievous crime to take advantage of the vulnerability and innocence of youth as a way of making profits. In the church we ought to be about the business of targeting our youth to make prophets, not profits.

Eutychus: Tuning Out, Dropping Out

A third portrait of youth in the early church is found in Acts 20:7-12, the story of Eutychus. Young people have a way of creating excitement in the most mundane situations. This young man Eutychus dozes off and falls out a window because Paul has preached for many hours.

Why did he fall asleep? Was he making an earnest effort to participate in the believers' fellowship but lacking the attention span to keep pace with the others? Was he just bored because Paul preached too long? Had he eaten too much food, which made him sluggish and sleepy? After all, the believers had gathered in the house for the purpose of breaking bread and eating.

Whatever the explanation for it, his sleeping leads to his death, so what might have been a laughing matter quickly turns to tragedy. Young Eutychus causes great excitement by falling out of the window, but the greatest excitement of all comes when God works a miracle of resurrection through Paul. The man of God seems to take the whole thing in stride. He stretches himself over the lifeless boy and embraces him back to life. Then Paul marches right back upstairs, eats and keeps on talking until the sun comes up! A tragic situation is transformed into a demonstration of God's power, and the people are greatly comforted.

Lessons and Warnings

What lessons can the youth of today learn from the youth of the New Testament church? Rhoda was a young girl with more enthusiasm than good sense. Youthful enthusiasm is a great gift to the church, particularly in its worship and music, but enthusiasm must be balanced with wisdom. Also, for credibility's sake, it is important to make sure that testimony matches up with evidence.

The anonymous slave girl was exploited by evil spirits and prostituted by money-hungry spiritual pimps. If young Christians can position themselves to be used by the God who loves them, then they will not have to worry about being exploited by those who despise them. And if others do abuse and exploit, God is still able to work it all out for good. We are not told what happened to the slave girl after her deliverance, but we do know that God brought deliverance to both the prisoners and their jailer, as a consequence of Paul and Silas's persistent praise in times of persecution.

Eutychus's story can be taken as a warning to young people not to tune out and drop out when the congregation is worshiping and the minister is preaching. Today's youth may not be in danger of literally falling and breaking their necks if they allow themselves to be overwhelmed with boredom, but the consequences of tuning out teaching and preaching can indeed be disastrous to the mind, soul and spirit. If young people can be at the center of the commotion, at the center of the problem, as many observers in our modern society would say they indeed are, then by faith they can become the center of the solution.

God remains poised to do miraculous, life-changing things in the lives of young people today. And some of the young people God wants to choose and use are floundering at the center of the problem, full of enthusiasm but lacking in wisdom; being exploited, but not aware of it; dropping out of everything positive and dropping into everything negative out of sheer boredom with life. What Paul did when he raised Eutychus from the dead was the same miracle that Jesus performed at the funeral bier of the widow's son, the same miracle that the prophet Elijah did for the son of the widow of Zarepath and the same miracle that Elisha did for the son of the Shunammite woman. In each case there is a testimony of God's abiding readiness to do works of deliverance and healing for people of all ages.

PART IV
BREAKING DOWN BARRIERS
A Challenge to the Church

10
THE CHILDREN'S BREAD

But she came and knelt before him, saying,
"Lord, help me." He answered, "It is not fair to take
the children's food and throw it tothe dogs." She
said, "Yes, Lord, yet even the dogs eat the crumbs
that fall from their masters' table." Then
Jesus answered her, "Woman, great is your faith!
Let it be done for you as you wish." And her
daughter was healed instantly.
MATTHEW 15:25-28

*T*he story of the Canaanite woman tells of a mother who comes to Jesus on behalf of a child in trouble. Her main motive for seeking and conversing with Jesus is to get help for her child. But in the process of tracking Jesus down and confronting him with her request, she opens for him a whole new understanding of his own mission and of the people's capacity for faith development.

The Authority of Urgency
The Canaanite woman is willing to do whatever it takes to get Jesus' attention because she is seeking it not for her own benefit but on behalf of her demon-possessed child. One can imagine her coming in a manner typical of any mother who moves in response to her child's distress, with fire in her eyes, forcefulness in her steps and flex in her muscles. She refuses to be intercepted, interrupted or interdicted until she is satisfied that she has exhausted all avenues

and possibilities for getting help for her child. She approaches Jesus with the authority of urgency—compelled to bold, uninhibited, immediate action because of her deep sense of her child's distress and endangerment. The authority of urgency causes her to shout and cry out to him, to follow hard after Jesus, demanding a response from him.

It seems that this woman has received special grace to seek Jesus out in this way. Her encounter with Jesus occurs after he has already crossed the physical boundary separating Jew from Gentile. In fact, he is seeking a vacation or retreat, so to speak; his sojourn in Tyre and Sidon is intended to provide a sorely needed respite from his intense involvement with the Jews.

A Vision of Unity and Inclusion

The Canaanite woman seems to be guided by a vision of unity as she seeks healing for her daughter. She wants to be included in what Jesus is doing, to be a beneficiary of his ministry. But Jesus' initial response is silence. Moreover, the male disciples are so intent upon getting rid of her that they pressure Jesus to take action against her: "His disciples came and urged him, saying, 'Send her away, for she keeps shouting after us' " (Mt 15:23).

Why did these men want to distance themselves from this woman? Was it simply because she was female and they were all males? Was it because she was a Gentile and they were all Jews? Was it because she was a Canaanite, a member of an ethnic group historically identified as Israel's pagan enemies? Or was it because she was the parent of a hopelessly incurable child and their children were perfectly healthy and whole?

Despite whatever reasons these men may have had for rejecting her, the Canaanite woman realized that she and her daughter were a part of the kingdom of God. Perhaps it was her experience of suffering, of parenting under difficult circumstances, that moved her to envision herself and her family in union with the ministry of Jesus and his followers.

Jesus embraces the woman's vision of unity and grows in his

understanding of who is included in the gospel of the kingdom. This is the only occasion in the Gospels when Jesus actually loses an argument! He has said that he has been sent only to the lost sheep of Israel. He says that the children's bread should not be fed to dogs. Yet he is impressed with the woman's insight that those who are denied access to the whole loaf can nevertheless get a blessing from the crumbs.

Sometimes life is not fair. Sometimes because of racism, sexism, color prejudice or a host of other reasons, people don't get what they deserve or want or need in life. But rather than lamenting that she had been left out, this woman gently insists upon being included, because she sees the essential connection between her predicament and Jesus' power. She claims oneness with the very men who would have preferred that she go away. Having been denied access to the children's bread, she lays claim to the "crumbs."

Her faith, however, ultimately authorizes her to take a seat at the table, which represents God's provision for the needs of all children. Her dialogue with Jesus evokes the imagery of the most beloved psalm:

You prepare a table before me
in the presence of my enemies;
you anoint my head with oil;
my cup overflows. (Ps 23:5)

Can it be that God anointed this distressed mother to exemplify the principle of unity by pushing her way past the hostility, prejudice and narrow-mindedness of others in order to take her seat, by faith, at the kingdom feast where there is plenty for all? Certainly her faith is rewarded. Her daughter is healed as Jesus voices approval of her persistence in seeking divine intervention.

Unconditional Faith

The Canaanite woman's faith emerges with a peculiar quality forged under conditions of parental distress—it is unconditional faith. Unconditional love is impartial and undiminished by changes in circumstances or lack of merit; in the New Testament Greek this is known as *agapē* love. The unconditional faith of this mother means that she disregards the limitations, the doubts, the prejudices and fears people would impose upon her children, with the bold assurance that God has overruled every hindrance to their well-being and access to God's presence.

Many of us parents would claim to have unconditional love for our children, loving them regardless, in spite of, anyhow. But it is really our children who love unconditionally. They seem to come into this world knowing how to love us without criticizing, blaming or holding back—that is, until they learn from adults how to put conditions on their affections.

Jesus is impressed, overwhelmed actually, by this mother's faith. When she declares that "even dogs eat the crumbs that fall from their masters' table," she suggests that even if insulted, rejected, labeled unfavorably and categorized unfairly, she will not be denied. She is determined that her child will be blessed by God and made whole. Her unconditional faith enables her to hold out hope for her child's deliverance regardless of whether she is received as worthy of ministry. She connects her faith in God with her faith in her child's future.

So the child in trouble is transformed into a source of great blessing—when the mother's faith is unleashed, at that moment her child is completely healed. This is not to suggest that parents should blame themselves for not having enough faith whenever their children suffer illness or disability. Rather, the point is to acknowledge the importance of the human factor in the prophetic ministry and mission of Jesus.

The Canaanite woman's story is a powerful illustration of how ministry at the margins challenges and transforms the outlook of those at the center. Her faith is effective because she develops a sound strategy for breaking down barriers and traditions that otherwise would be left intact. The ethics of the gospel can be readily discerned in this story, as faith, hope and love converge in a mother's urgent and worshipful appeal for help, as well as in the demand for justice so that the special needs of children can be addressed without respect to race, ethnicity, sex or social status.

This mother's exemplary courage inspires hope for the children of today to be delivered from the traps of poverty, disease, despair and dysfunction through the compassionate, empathic concern of believers who are willing to hold themselves morally accountable to God and neighbor. Justice is the children's bread.

11

RECONCILIATION
Jesus at Jericho

Zacchaeus stood there and said to the Lord, "Look,

half of my possessions, Lord, I will give to the

poor; and if I have defrauded anyone of anything, I

will pay back four times as much."

LUKE 19:8

*T*he gospel of Jesus Christ is meaningless without reconciliation. The ministry of reconciliation is our collective commitment to overcome the barriers that divide and alienate people from each other by the healing power of love and unity that flows from the Spirit of God. The New Testament accounts of how Jesus ministered at the margins of his society provide a strong foundation for teaching, modeling and promoting reconciliation both in the academy and in the church.

Spirituality and Social Action
The exclusion and rejection of others on the basis of race, sex or class are symptoms of a grave spiritual disability. Spirituality, in simplest terms, means responsiveness to God. This understanding of spirituality finds application in worship, in interpersonal relationships and in the political and economic sphere. We can theologize all we want,

but until we begin to deal with the spiritual and ethical implications of our ideas about God, nothing will change. Our opinions about the nature of God may change and develop in time, but our obligation to emulate God's justice and mercy is permanent.

Our norms, values and moral principles must be consistent with our theology if we are to practice reconciliation with any measure of integrity. The experience of the holy necessarily draws us into communion with people whose race, sex and class differ from our own. In this regard, the true test of our spirituality is our responsiveness to the divine call to reconciliation and the divine mandate to love our neighbors. Christians too easily separate individual conversion from social transformation; if individuals can be changed by the gospel of Jesus Christ, why not also families, communities and nations?

When we move toward implementing a biblically based understanding of reconciliation, are we acting in accord with the will of God? Are we moving in the power of the Holy Spirit? Are we walking in the footsteps of Christ? On the other hand, when we reject or exclude others on the basis of race, sex, culture or class, can we claim divine authority and anointing for our actions?

The relevance of reconciliation, spirituality and social action to gospel ethics can be illustrated with reference to three texts taken from the Gospel of Luke, all having to do with Jesus in the ancient city of Jericho. Jericho was on a major trade route and was an important customs center. Much of Jesus' ministry among marginalized people occurred in cities like Jericho, and his words and work in the urban environment speak to the problem of multicultural ministry and urban mission in our own time.

Zacchaeus: Reconciliation with the Poor

One person Jesus encountered in Jericho was Zacchaeus (Lk 19:1-10). He was a rich tax collector who gained his wealth by exploiting his own people using the racially and economically oppressive "system" to his advantage, and they apparently resented the role he played in their economic suffering. But when Jesus called him down from the tree, down from his lofty position of power and wealth, he was also calling him to account for his sin. Salvation came to Zacchaeus when he took the initiative to be reconciled with his neighbors by making restitution of what he had stolen from them.

Evidently Jericho, like my own city of Washington, D.C., was a city of extremes—extremely rich and extremely poor. So this reconciliation is significant because a rich man sought reconciliation with the poor, in addition to the other taxpayers he had exploited. In the presence of Zacchaeus Jesus affirmed his own divine calling to seek and save the lost. Let us never assume that it is only the urban poor who are lost and need to be reconciled to God.

The Blind Beggar: Persistent Spirituality

On the outskirts of Jericho, Jesus encounters a blind beggar, in contrast to the urban-suburban demographics of our time which usually posits the poor in the inner city and the affluent outside the city:

> As he approached Jericho, a blind man was sitting by the roadside begging. When he heard a crowd going by, he asked what was happening. They told him, "Jesus of Nazareth is passing by." Then he shouted, "Jesus, Son of David, have mercy on me!" (Lk 18:35-38)

Spirituality is an issue here, on several levels. First, we observe that the blind man exercised his sense of hearing to discern that he needed to be included in what was happening around him. He may have been blind, but he wasn't hard of hearing. Woe to those of us who will neither see nor hear! His spirituality, his responsiveness, did not end with his questioning the crowd. He began to shout. Perhaps he was one of those loud, disruptive people whose worship style and demeanor are despised by those who have a more culturally refined approach to religion. The people tried to silence him, but he persisted in his shouting. Deep spirituality is a *persistent* pattern of being focused, attentive and responsive to the presence of God in our lives; it is also a willingness to invoke God's help.

Jesus stopped and ordered that the man be brought to him. When

Jesus spoke to him, the man was ready to answer, and to ask for his sight to be restored. In other words, he had already assessed his own neediness before the Lord. And Jesus declared that it was the man's faith that saved him.

The story ends with the man following Jesus and glorifying God, in itself a wonderful prescription for a life of spiritual discipline. Maybe now he was making more noise than at the beginning, but instead of silencing him the people praised God with him, because of him. In this instance spirituality bridged the gap between Jesus and the man who needed the blessing of sight, between the boisterous beggar and the contemptuous crowd, between those with seen and unseen disabilities. When healing occurs and barriers are overcome, God is glorified.

The Good Samaritan: Empathy Across Barriers

The third text is the parable of the good Samaritan; "A man was going down from Jerusalem to Jericho, and fell into the hands of robbers, who stripped him, beat him, and went away, leaving him half dead" (Lk 10:30). This is a story about the hazardous road between Jericho and Jerusalem, told by Jesus to answer a lawyer's question about who is qualified to be treated as neighbor. The hypothetical Samaritan is presented as culturally inferior but ethically superior to the religious experts and leaders, because he is a model of social action. He enacts the ethics of the gospel by disregarding racial, religious and cultural barriers in his determination to show mercy to a stranger in need. His commitment to social action is quite costly, requiring serious personal investments of time, effort and money.

Jesus gives an ethical answer to the lawyer's question concerning eternal life: "Go and do likewise" (v. 37). In other words, do the same thing as the Good Samaritan, and you will have eternal life. What makes the Samaritan morally "good" is his willingness to put himself in the other person's shoes, that is, to have empathy for his neighbor, despite the many risks involved. Then he treats that neighbor with compassion, to the end of healing wounds.

There is a song from the traditional music of the African-American slaves that includes a joyful commentary on the Old Testament Jericho: "Joshua fit [fought] de battle of Jericho, and the walls came tumbling down." The song reminds us that the biblical Jericho was a city with walls. When Jesus came to Jericho, walls still stood in the way of reconciliation and human wholeness, but they came tumbling down once spiritual renewal was merged with social action.

12
MINISTRY & MISSION IN MULTICULTURAL PERSPECTIVE

Then Peter began to speak to them: "I truly understand

that God shows no partiality, but in every nation

anyone who fears him and does what is right is

acceptable to him."

ACTS 10:34-35

*T*here is a widespread perception that racial and cultural differences have an impact on who gets equity, access to resources,
recognition and the like in Christian educational institutions. The
problem, simply stated, is that African-Americans, Asian-Americans,
Hispanics and other so-called minorities are increasingly in a position to compete with whites not only for the resources these institutions have to offer but also for positions of power from which to
exercise their gifts and authority as educators, administrators and
managers of institutional structures.

Once those persons who have traditionally been excluded become
included—that is, gain access and equity in these settings—the
focus of attention shifts to another level of questioning and concern.
For example, what norms and values and rules should be employed
as a guide to the exercise of power? Is it better to assimilate the ethics
of the dominant culture or to do things differently? Should so-called

minorities distance themselves from other "minorities" as a necessary step toward feeling included by the majority and minimizing feelings of being different? Or should an aggressive, dissenting posture of advocacy be maintained, in a constant struggle on behalf of others who have yet to experience the privileges of access and equity? Once a person feels included, does he or she then serve the best interests of the organization by acting to exclude others? Who ultimately benefits from multicultural efforts and emphases? What actual value is ascribed to diversity within evangelical Christian institutions? And if we value diversity, what meaning does unity have?

A Reconciled Community

The ministry of reconciliation is fundamental to the Christian faith. It is no accident that the Spirit chose an international, multicultural gathering of believers in Jerusalem as the setting for the Pentecost outpouring, whose testimony was that "in our own languages we hear them speaking about God's deeds of power" (Acts 2:11). Pentecost is God's remedy for disunity. Many languages, many colors, many cultures, but one testimony of one God.

Pentecost does not homogenize the people of God; rather, it recognizes the value of diversity. But our racism hinders us from appreciating cultural diversity for what it is and blinds us to the fact that the revelation of God is not exclusive to any one race or color or language. The gift of the Holy Spirit was designed to be poured out on all flesh, all nations, but the Spirit poured out testifies that God desires for all peoples to be united in our praise of God, by the power of God, and not by our manipulation of privilege based on race, sex or class. If you are my Christian brother or sister, then include me because of my testimony and not because of my degree of conformity to your culture or comfort zones. Cultural difference is no legitimate basis for exclusion from the body of believers, and cultural conformity alone is no legitimate basis for inclusion in the body of believers.

The Christian church is a consensus community built around the person of Jesus Christ, and the confession that Jesus is Lord. The gospel of Jesus Christ is that in him we find power to be saved from our sins, healed from our diseases, delivered from the things that bind us, and set free to know and to do God's will as we commit ourselves to serving human need. And anyone who has believed and received that gospel as good news is automatically joined to an ancient and eternal consensus community of fellowship with the Son of God.

The following is an interpretation of two passages of Scripture that together demonstrate the evolution of an ethics of the gospel and describe its impact on the early church as an emergent multicultural faith community. They are Peter's confession of Christ (Mt 16:13-23) and the conversion of Cornelius, when Peter confesses the impartial God (Acts 10:1-8, 34-48).

Who Do You Say That I Am?

The scene of Peter's first confession at Caesarea Philippi begins when Jesus initiates a public opinion survey concerning his own identity. But after surveying the people's opinions, he makes a much more pointed inquiry to his inner circle of followers: "Who do you say that I am?"

Peter confesses that Jesus is the Christ, the Anointed One of God. And Jesus responds by claiming this revelation as the evidence of the divine enlightenment that shall be forever the foundation of the good news community, which is the church. With this divine enlightenment comes divine empowerment, the keys of the kingdom of heaven, authority to bind and loose.

That authority of binding and loosing includes the church's authority to engage in the binding and loosing of people's thinking. It seems that for every example of a person or group that uses brainwashing, indoctrination and mind control games to exploit people and keep them in line, there are others who encourage educational and intellectual development so that people are nurtured for growth rather than stunted in their ignorance.

God revealed to Peter the true identity of Jesus, but who do modern evangelical Christians say he is? What is his relevance to the multicultural enterprise? What color is Jesus? Can a Savior be black?

In modern-day America, *black* as a racial designation is a combination of color, culture and condition. Black is actually a broad range of colors, because of the way race is defined in this country. In America black means "not white," in the sense of not having 100 percent white ancestry, even if your hair is blond, your eyes blue and your skin the palest shade imaginable. Given that the Bible gives us no indication that Jesus had any ancestral roots in Europe, there is no way we can designate him as white in today's terms, notwithstanding the images created by Michelangelo, Leonardo da Vinci and other great white masters. On the basis of current criteria, if the historical Jesus were to appear in the flesh in America today, he would definitely not be classified as white.

Culturally, we have a similar situation. The Bible gives no indication of Jesus' having any European cultural influences. He was a Palestinian Jew who spent some undetermined number of his early years in Egypt, and Egypt is on the continent now designated as Africa. With regard to blackness as a social condition, in this country historically we identify blackness with suffering, with undeserved victimization because of the racism of the people in power.

Jesus was born into poverty and lived his life in relationship with the poor, who become the special focus of his preaching, teaching and healing ministry. Yet when Jesus told Peter and the others that he must suffer at the hands of the religious leaders and be killed, Peter rebuked him, refusing to accept this portrayal of the Lord. Jesus in turn rebuked Peter with perhaps the harshest words we find him using in the Scriptures. Peter the rock becomes Peter the stumbling block, having strayed from the path of divine revelation to dwell on the human element rather than the divine.

The point here is to show that like Peter, we can become so enamored of a particular view of Jesus that we close our minds to what Jesus is saying about who and what he really is. The image of a white Jesus that many of us find comfortable and appropriate does not match up with the biblical record of who Jesus was. And we cannot resolve the matter by saying that the color of Jesus doesn't make any difference, especially if what is really being communicated is the sentiment that it doesn't make any difference as long as it's white. Color is not the only issue here; it is also entirely inappropriate and unscriptural to ascribe to Jesus the cultural biases and middle-class identity of the typical white American Christian.

If we can move beyond the image of a white Jesus in our thinking and our faith, perhaps then we can envision some of the deeper challenges of multicultural approaches to Christian community, where the question of who should be included in our existing structures is a mere starting point. The real issue is who is included in the divine scheme of things, in the kingdom of God that Jesus preached and died for, and our accountability before God for our relationships with people who are racially different from us.

God Shows No Partiality

Peter's "second" confession takes place in Caesarea, at the home of the Roman centurion Cornelius, as recorded in Acts 10:1-8, 34-48. The key passage begins with verse 34: "Then Peter began to speak to them: 'I truly understand that God shows no partiality, but in every nation anyone who fears him and does what is right is acceptable to him.' " The concept of race is not mentioned in this passage or anywhere else in the Bible as a category. But it is clear that the controversy in the early church with regard to who was included in and who excluded from what God was doing in the world came to a head when Peter encountered a European—a white Gentile male— who wanted to be saved and filled with the Holy Ghost.

Can a white man be saved? Cornelius is often regarded as the first Gentile convert to Christianity, and the manifestation of the Holy Spirit to Cornelius and his household is referred to as the Second Pentecost, or the Gentile Pentecost. But note that God was making the same statement in the second Pentecost as in the first: that the Spirit is destined to be poured out on all peoples, people from all nations, and since God has no prejudice or partiality toward one group over another, neither should we.

According to the chronology of Acts, however, Cornelius was not the first Gentile convert in the early church. That distinction may belong to the Ethiopian eunuch, the court official who met Philip on the desert road, received the gospel of Jesus Christ, was baptized and went on his way back to Ethiopia rejoicing (Acts 8:26-39). Maybe Cornelius gets the credit due to his high military rank and wealth, as indicated by the fact that he owned slaves. When Peter asks, "Can anyone withhold the water for baptizing thesë people who have received the Holy Spirit just as we have?" (Acts 10:47), he raises the same question as was posed by the Ethiopian convert in Acts 8:36— "What is to prevent me from being baptized?" The answer in both cases is, not race, not culture, not class!

Peter struggled after his first confession to accept the prediction that the Anointed One would suffer at the hands of the religious leaders, and Jesus rebuked him for it. But the second confession, also based upon a revelation from God, provoked divine approbation as the gift of the Holy Spirit was poured out upon everyone assembled. In other words, it was only after Peter overcame his own exclusive biases and ignorant prejudice that the way was made clear for Cornelius to be saved, baptized and filled with the Holy Spirit. God is magnified by the word of impartiality and justice.

We can only speculate as to whether or not Cornelius remained a military man and a slaveholder after he became saved. What we do know for certain from these readings is that God condemns racial and cultural prejudice, and only those who fear God and do justice are acceptable to God. Once Peter accepted his mission to Cornelius, the racial and cultural barriers to the gospel fell. His story offers a model for multicultural ministry in our own time.

One God, One Race, One Message

Further light on this notion of multicultural ministry is found in the high-priestly prayer of Jesus recorded in John 17. In particular, three aspects of Christian unity can be discerned in the words Jesus offered on behalf of his followers—a *message*, a *means* and a *manifestation.*

Unity as a message. First, the message, simply stated, is that we all are invited into fellowship with God through Jesus Christ. If we believe in him, we have eternal life in God. The Christian message is really not any more complicated than that. Yet it is only through the sharing of this message that others can know about Christ and believe that he has been sent from God. God sent Jesus, Jesus sent his disciples, and the commission has been passed on to every succeeding generation of discipled believers.

This message is for the world. It may be shaped and honed and rehearsed in the pulpits and classrooms of the church, but it is intended for the world. Once any one of us receives and believes it, our obligation is to pass it on.

The prayer, then, is for the unity of the message, that the word we share, the gospel we preach, the message we bear might be one powerful proclamation of who Jesus is for the world. It is this one message that unites Christians as one people of one God.

Unity as a means. Second, in this prayer unity is a means to an end, and not an end in itself:

I ask not only on behalf of these, but also on behalf of those who will believe in me through their word, that they may all be one.

As you, Father, are in me and I am in you, may they also be in us, so that the world may believe that you have sent me. (Jn 17:20-21)

It is good for Christians in local churches and on college campuses to engage in interdenominational efforts to foster Christian unity. But unity should not be lifted up as an end in itself. Neither should multiculturalism be regarded as an end in itself, nor diversity, nor inclusiveness. Rather, these are means toward the end that no one be *excluded* from what God is doing in our midst, or from the resources God has made available through Christian institutions and organizations.

We must cultivate an awareness of how racism, sexism, ignorance and prejudice delude Christians into excluding others from vital spheres of God's blessing and work. The true end or purpose of our efforts to overcome these barriers is the acknowledgment that God made us all and loves us all as bearers of God's divine image. And special programs and efforts are needed just as long as blind and narrow-minded people refuse to believe, practice or honor this end of making sure no one gets excluded from what God is doing.

It is essential here to underscore the point that the multicultural impetus should not be understood as merely an effort to include "minorities and women" in what a particular church or campus is doing, but rather should be representative of the intention of us all to be included in what *God* is doing. So we should not congratulate ourselves just for coming together across the boundaries of race, sex and culture. It is better to envision Christian unity as a platform for demonstrating the power of God's Spirit, the purpose of God's creation and the preeminence of God's Son. The purpose of unity, the end of unity, is that the world would become convinced and encouraged to believe in Jesus Christ.

Unity as a manifestation. Third, unity is a manifestation of God's glory, not ours. When the world sees people of diverse cultures and skin colors, rich and poor, male and female, young and old, coming together as one family, then they will know God has done it. We do not create unity in the body of Christ—God has already done that from the beginning. Our responsibility is to maintain the unity God has created and to be vigilant against all the forces that work actively to keep us separated and at odds with each other. There is but one God, and we all are bearers of God's image. God is glorified when people begin to see and understand that our human worth in the sight of God is not determined by our color, our culture, our sex or our income.

Will American Christians ever learn to affirm that we are really one human family? Will it ever be possible for us to celebrate differences in skin color as evidence of the divine artistry of creation and not as grounds for continued hatred, exploitation and prejudice?

Genuine unity, not tokenism, is a manifestation of what God has done to make us one. The word of truth that Jesus lifted up in his prayer remains the ongoing mandate for the Christian mission to the world. It is this truth that binds us together, by one message of unity in Jesus Christ, by one means to a clearly understood end of genuine inclusiveness in community, and by one glorious manifestation of God's revelation in Jesus Christ, entrusted to one church, margin to center.

EPILOGUE

Urban Ministry & Prophetic Mission: The Autobiography of Reverend Hattie Downer

he Reverend Dr. Hattie Downer is a woman whose lifetime of ministry and mission is exemplary of the Christian ideals and imperatives set forth in this book. She was born in Columbia, South Carolina, in 1914 and as a teenager migrated with her family to New York City in 1928. At that time she began assisting her mother, the Reverend Ivory Downer, in establishing Sunday schools, planting churches and carrying on the work of urban evangelism and outreach. From 1945 to 1955 she served as the national youth field worker for the National Association of the Church of God, an organization of predominantly black Church of God congregations that convenes annually in West Middlesex, Pennsylvania. This position required her to travel throughout the United States organizing and conducting ministries for children and youth. Subsequently she was commissioned by the Board of Church Extension and Home Missions of the Church of God (Anderson, Indiana) as she continued her field work in the southern United States.

In 1973, following the death of her mother, she became pastor of the Williamsburg Community Church of God in Brooklyn, New York. The next year the church, known also as the "Cathedral of Joy," moved from a storefront to a large building that could better accommodate a variety of outreach ministries. In 1987 the Reverend Downer was awarded an honorary doctorate by Anderson University in recognition of the fact that she has served a wide range of desperate human needs with innovation, courage and perseverance, and that under her leadership the Cathedral of Joy became a redemptive haven for the powerless, hopeless and homeless and a ministry center for Anderson students doing urban missions assignments under her supervision.

What follows is a first-person narrative of Hattie Downer's spiritual pilgrimage. Her story is presented here as an embodiment of the ethics of the gospel as outlined in this book. She describes a lifetime dedicated to proclamation of the good news of God's reign in the world and implementation of righteousness and justice in people's lives. Her pursuit of education, employment and a call to ministry as a black woman in twentieth-century America recalls the struggles of women who experienced divine empowerment in spite of their disadvantaged position in the biblical world. She speaks specifically of what it is like to be led of the Spirit in partnership with men and women of God who are determined to serve human needs in the light of God's righteousness and justice.

Although Hattie Downer never married or had children of her own, she perfected the practice of community parenting as an effective means of outreach to children and youth in the urban environment. She succeeded in sustaining multicultural ministries and partnerships years before diversity became "fashionable." This firsthand account of one woman's fulfillment of her call to ministry, despite the hardships imposed by poverty, racial discrimination and sexual bias, demonstrates that the unifying and empowering gospel of Jesus Christ is yet at work "at the margins."

Beginnings: Columbia, South Carolina
I was born on September 21, 1914, the sixth child of my parents, and

the only one born in the city. We lived at 914 Divine Street in Columbia, South Carolina. My father was Early Downer, and my mother was Ivory Virginia Smith Downer. My oldest sister Ruth and my oldest brother Daniel were born in Athens, Georgia. My mother and father moved back to Columbia after the two older ones were born, and Priscilla, Joe and Bessie were born in the country where my grandmother had a house, in Lykesland, South Carolina, a suburb of Columbia.

My father had a "pressing club," what they would call a tailor shop now. He used gasoline one day with the hot iron to do his pressing, and he wasn't aware that the house was going to catch on fire. And this little baby Hattie had to be put out the window, and somebody had to catch me; that's when they told me that I was almost gone, because the house burned down. So that was the end of living there. We had to move back to the country where my grandmother was. So we had another little sister to be born down there, and they called her Abby—her real name was Lydia—and that was number seven. The last child was a sister. Her name was Ivory Virginia—she was named for my mother. In all my mother had eight children.

They moved from the country to other parts of South Carolina where my mother and father tried to do some farming, but they didn't take to that too well. I can barely remember that; I must have been three or four years old. I do remember that I was a little girl and I didn't like to keep my clothes on because it always got too hot!

My father and mother had a mule named Blue. My brother took sick, and Priscilla, my third sister, was a little girl, and she kicked the mule and the mule kicked her in the face. That was one of the tragedies. Mother and Father didn't know about going to the doctor and seeing that she was taken care of properly. She carried that through her life, and she lived to be eighty-one years old. It left a scar on her, and she never did feel right about that; she thought it was a bad thing for her.

Early and Ivory Downer
My father started a school at night among adults in a small town in

South Carolina. He was a very avid educator, and he wanted to teach people about God and about reading and writing. He was born February 23, 1884, in Elverton, Georgia, and as a boy he always wanted to be a preacher. So he used to preach funerals for birds and dogs. And he was a strict Methodist. They gave him an opportunity to preach from the time he was sixteen. I don't know how much formal education he had, but he was very smart. He told us that his mother had wanted a little girl when he was born, and she named him Pearl. And when he went to school and told the teacher his name, she told him, "No, that's a girl's name. You're going to be Earl." He put the "Earl-*y*" there himself.

My mother was born August 17, 1876, and she died in July 1973, a few weeks before she would have been ninety-seven. She was a Methodist like my father. She talked of how the white and black saints were together in worship, because the saints from the North and from the West came through South Carolina and all the southern states, and they were evangelizing all that old, first-generation Church of God. My mother heard the gospel from Brother Lundy and others, men and women, white and black together, who were preaching. And when she heard the gospel, she said goodby to her mama, her sister, her cousins; she told them, "Goodby, I'm gone," and left the Methodist church. The text that caught her attention was Ephesians 4: "one Lord, one faith, one baptism, one Father of us all, who is above us all and in you all." And she said that oneness got her, she wanted to be in that.

My father got into the Church of God under similar circumstances—the saints came through, and he got saved. And they worshiped in Columbia together until the authorities separated them, because they were not ready for the races to be together. The Church of God could have been working together better for a long time, but the police frightened them.

My mother and father met at the Church of God camp meeting in Augusta, Georgia in 1903. They fell in love and were married in 1904, and in 1905 they had their first child. In the Church of God then you didn't court any long time, you just got married if that was what you wanted. And they had no alternative—they just got married, this was what they wanted. And he was much younger than she, very young—I don't know why they married! I don't know whether he was twenty-one or not, but she was twenty-eight at that time. They must have had a reception or something for them down in the country, in South Carolina. Then he took her back to their home in Athens, Georgia, where they had had the wedding, and that's where the first two children were born.

My mother was a seamstress in her youth. My mother and her sister went to Allen University, which was related to the African Methodist Episcopal Church; they were very well-educated women.

My father became a pastor; I can remember some of the churches he pastored away from home. He was the janitor of old Howard School in Columbia, a public school. And that meant he had to prepare the school for the next day. In the winter he had to take out the ashes and bring up coal for all the rooms, and there were a lot of rooms on each floor. He had to help get the fire started in the building. There was a stove in each room, and a scuttle (bucket) of coal had to be placed by each stove overnight in the winter. And he also was the lunch man. When I was a little child he would make these sandwiches, salmon and cheese with bread, and he would wrap them and bring them to school. The children would buy them for a nickel or a dime. That's the way he made money to help us to survive. I used to look at those sandwiches and smell that salmon, and wanted some, but he wouldn't give us any of it. That's all the children would have to eat, the sandwiches he brought.

We lived on a street called Railroad Avenue. After I went to school, I was old enough to stay after school to help him clean up and to get things together.

Preaching Parents

My brothers and sisters and I helped to work at the school, because my father was on the road so much. He was an evangelist who got called to revivals. Then there was the pioneer work in South Carolina—they started churches in small towns like Miley and Barnville and places like that. There were certain churches where he and my mother would go and work. She also was a pastor. She went to a little place where a lady got saved and a crowd of children—eventually she moved to Columbia. This sister was a blessing, for later in life she became a nurse. We sent for her in New York to help take care of my mother in her old age.

When I was born, my mother was already preaching. She told us about how they were having meetings in Augusta or Sumter, wherever the big meetings were, and my mother was pregnant with one of us, and she was about to preach. Brother Harmon, one of the older, senior ministers in that day, stopped her and said, "No, Ivory, the Lord doesn't want you to preach, not in that condition."

So she said, "Well, Lord, I can't preach," but the Lord told her she could pray. And she did a powerful piece of praying. She was a good preacher—she was an evangelistic preacher; the Lord used her a lot.

They traveled by train, by wagon. They didn't have too many buses or cars. Eventually my father got a Model T Ford, and he would go back and forth to Jenkinsville to pastor. My mother and father pastored there at a certain times. A lot of people got saved up there. My father pastored in Waynesboro, Jenkinsville, down in the lower part of South Carolina, in Richmond, Virginia, and in St. Petersburg, Florida. He didn't travel back and forth to Richmond and St. Petersburg. He lived there and commuted, and once in a while he would come back home. My mother consistently stayed at home.

A Different World: New York City

In 1927 my oldest brother was lured away from Columbia with a distant cousin, and no one knew where he was. My mother finally found out where he was and went to New York in 1927 or 1928 to find him, and she found him. And he was very sick. During the year 1928 my mother sent for Priscilla and Joe. My oldest sister Ruth had married, and she had a little baby girl. Ruth, Priscilla and Joe came to New York. That left Bessie, Abby and myself down in Columbia.

We had to walk to school a long walk. Abby was smart—she was always winning prizes for spelling bees and math, and she could answer things just like that, off the top of her head. My mother knew this couple who were coming to New York. And she had written to us and said get things together "because we are going to send for you to come up to New York." And we were so happy, because we three youngest girls were down there by ourselves. And the people who came for us were supposed to be Christians, but they didn't have the flavor like we had been raised in a Christian home.

There were seven or eight people in a car, and we motored to New York. We had locked up the house. Finally we were reunited with the other part of the family in New York in 1928. Because I was shy and frightened as a child, I was so glad to be with my mother and I just cried.

"Now," Mama said, "now, don't cry. You're here with Mama now and you don't have to cry." And I *was* a big girl. But I was so glad; I hadn't seen my mother since early in the year, and here it was going toward the fall. And all of us were happy.

But being in New York was a different world to little children living in the city by themselves. We were very conscious of knowing who we were—we were church-related children, and we loved the Lord and all like that—but New York was a different world. Some of the saints in New York let my mother have a railroad flat at 141 Jefferson Avenue in Brooklyn. Sister and Brother Lay lived on Putnam Avenue, the next street from us. They became like shepherds over us, seeing about the family, seeing that everything was all right.

You had to get close together to live. When you came to New York from the South, you just had to cram together because people lived in a small space. We didn't have much room. The bathtub was not a bathtub; it was a tub you washed clothes in. You had to climb in to take your bath. It was fun. Anyway, we managed to do well, and we finally moved from there.

My younger sister and I went to Public School #3. Priscilla and Bessie went to Girls' High School. The sad part about it is that neither my mother nor my father was home when we had to start school in September. My sister was so smart that when they asked her a lot of questions she answered them and got in her right grade.

But I didn't know what to do, scared and frightened, all these people white and black and I didn't know how to react properly. I had been promoted to the eighth grade, but they put me back to the seventh. The lady talked like she wanted to put me back further than that. But after a while I learned how to talk a lot.

Church-Centered Life

When I got out of the eighth grade and we moved to 21 Sumter Street, that's where my mother started the church work. The winter of 1928, really in December and then January of 1929, was when we started the storefront. She found a place to live in the back of a storefront that she made into a church. She said the Lord told her that she had been worrying about her son, who was so sick, and the Lord said, "What about saving one man, and a nation perish?" She said the Lord spoke to her about so many people that were coming North and had nowhere to worship. So she just opened it up, and the saints from different places came to worship there.

I was comfortable going to school with the children, white and black together, though I never had gone to interracial schools before. But in those days there were very few blacks going to school in New York. In the area where we lived there wasn't an influx of blacks. There weren't too many in any of our classes, even when I went to Girls' High School. They started coming in after that; these were Depression years, so in the thirties there came more and more blacks.

We lived in the back of the place where we worshiped. My mother would cook, and on Sundays the people would come to church and there would be a family dinner already prepared for everybody to share. This is the way she lived in the South; anyone could come and get in on it. In fact, in the South they just called our home "the saints' home": anybody could just come and stay overnight or eat at our table. Even in Brooklyn they did.

We had a lady called Sister Lillie Bates—I won't ever forget her. She was from the South, and she stayed with us awhile. She had been in an accident, so my mother made room for her to live with us. And she was quite surprised at the way my mother kept us working and doing stuff all the time. She said, "Sister Ivory, when do you let these children play and have some fun?" We had never heard of that! We had fun, but no planned pleasure.

My oldest brother passed. He had rheumatic heart disease. He would go back and forth to Kings County Hospital. And after he died, my youngest sister passed, during the thirties. She was very smart. When she finished grammar school, they put her in what they called the "Rapid Advanced." They didn't have to go through the whole seventh, eighth and ninth grade. She went from her public school to junior high school, and she graduated. She was a poet. She made up a beautiful poem when she got ready to graduate. She didn't get to go to her graduation, though. She was very, very sick. But she made up her poem. She said she was going to go to stately Girls' High. But she didn't get to go. She went into the hospital, and she died. My sister died before my grandfather. That's the part I got so upset about. I said, "Oh God, why her and not my grandfather?"

On a Sunday we would go to Jamaica, New York. One of the ministers was trying to start a work in Jamaica. And my mother would go back and forth to help them. There was a streetcar, and they had just started building the "A" train subway. And someone asked my grandmother, "Grandma, what would you like to ride on, the elevator, the streetcar or the subway? They've got a new subway."

She said, "Well, I'll tell you. The streetcar is too much like home. And the subway is too much like going to hell. Take me on the 'up' train." She preferred going on the "el."

The Depression Years: Poverty and Discrimination

My mother needed help in paying the rent and taking care of us. I was the one that was home to help her, I was in high school. She would make little pies, and she sold those pies for a nickel. And I would be the one outside selling them. We had an old china closet that was dedicated to put the pies in to show the people. We would bring it out the store and put it on the sidewalk. And people would pass by and buy them.

Now this was in the terrible Depression era, when nickels were all you really would get. If a person gave you a dime and said, "Keep the change," that was very good, because that meant you got a nickel more. But we made money enough to help pay the rent for the storefront, and also to help the family. And I was the salesman.

During that time, seeing people, even though I wasn't fully aware of the humanity of the people, the humanness, the dire poverty and the sickness that I saw on faces—I didn't understand it. I saw these people were coming in from work or looking for work, and they were terribly distressed or depressed. But I would often say, "Oh, I hope when I have to go out, I won't look like that. I want to get a job and make some money so that I can help." This selling I was doing was nothing, but I had in my mind a vision of seeing something happen that was better for us.

After high school I went to look for a job. Four or five of us white and black kids went because we heard jobs were available somewhere. At that time we went to this place, and they said no jobs. When we black girls left, they called the white girls back.

I really didn't recognize discrimination and racial stuff until Martin Luther King's time, and I was an old woman then. So many things happened to get me involved to see racism. It was dawning on me because I wasn't quite as aware as I am now. In the South they were lynching, and there were atrocities done to blacks that were not supposed to be. A lot of women would be hurt and mauled by white people, but they would say a black did it. They would kill any black that came in their sight. So black men had a very horrible time. Many left the South with their families because they were just marked men. If they found you on the street, they'd kill you. That bothered me. And another thing, talking about racism, was the Scottsboro Boys. That was a case that went for years and years before we left the South and after we got up here, the Scottsboro Boys were a case like that Mr. Rodney King out there in California—something that was held before people, and they knew that they had done nothing but they were going to lynch them anyway. That was one of the cases that helped us to see racism in the South.

Graduating from Girls' High School, I wasn't able to go directly to Brooklyn College although there was no charge except for laboratory fee, which was fifteen dollars. You could go to school in Brooklyn if you lived in Brooklyn. But my mother didn't have the fifteen dollars, so I couldn't go. My two friends came by for me. Myrtle and Velma and I were very good friends, and they went to register at Brooklyn College and I was supposed to go with them, but I didn't go that night. I went later, but it was really a lot later. And Brooklyn College then was not the Brooklyn College as it is now, with the new buildings and everything. It was in downtown Brooklyn. But I didn't have the money to go at that time; we were just poor. And it didn't bother me so much; I just got hurt because I couldn't go with the girls. But I understood our condition, so it was one of those things.

In 1935 I had gotten out of school, and I was quite an older person to be coming out of high school so late. But they were encouraging us to stay in school, because so many of the children were dropping out of school, white and black, because of the Depression. So I stuck it out. And I got out of school, and I started helping my mother with the rent and all. I got jobs working in households, domestic work, helping my sisters Bessie and Priscilla.

A New Deal and Open Doors

President Roosevelt established the National Youth Administration Act, called the NYA. He had what he called a "Brain Trust" that helped him make up all these alphabets for the different agencies that he had made up in the government. Most of them are abolished, but some of them are still existing. The NYA and CCC, and those that were connected with young people, were taken out. In his "Brain Trust" he had hired this woman, Mary McLeod Bethune, who was the head of Bethune-Cookman College. She came to New York during these Depression years. It was like now when we try to get somebody to go around and encourage young people to stay in school. And I can remember very well the very place we were to listen to her. So she was telling us, "Boys and girls, the doors may be closed now, but they are going to open. And when they open, I want to tell you to be prepared to walk in those doors. Because when they're open, if you're prepared, you can walk in. For what you get in your brain, in your mind, no one can take from you. It's yours, and you have to use it."

She poured in some enthusiasm in my mind, because I wanted somebody to help me think, *I can do it.* That spurred me on. When Mrs. Bethune talked to us and gave us this fiery, enthusiastic encouragement, she pleaded with the boys and girls: "Stay in school, don't get out; if you don't have to, don't get out; be able to walk through the doors, I'm explaining to you, the doors will open." So OK, I'm waiting for the doors to open.

And the doors did open after World War II, when all the things happened that got the colored and white working. The reason I got that job was because my father was on WPA; he was working on public works, and then he left. When he left, I got this job with NYA. They gave us two or three days a week, half-days, and they gave us eleven dollars a week. That was good for a youngster who had nothing, to say "That's my money." So we all felt very proud of that.

And I worked at the YWCA on Ashland Place in Brooklyn, with the manager of the "Y," helping her in the office. They had an employment agency there. So sometimes in the evening they asked me would I stay a couple of hours, instead of coming early—come a little later and stay and answer the phone, because no one would be there. So I would answer the phone, and jobs would come for girls to come and serve dinner, or come to do certain types of work. And some of those jobs I took. I answered the phone and said, "All right, we'll have somebody there." And I was the person to go there! That was one strategy of negotiation I did on my own.

I went to the Business School at the "Y" in Manhattan on 135th Street, and I learned quite a few things—business, English, math, steno, typing—and I did well. And I got a job with the New York City Taxation and Assessment Bureau in the Municipal Building in Manhattan. In that job I made a salary of twenty-five dollars a week. I went to Brooklyn College for a year or two before I went to business school. It was like a crash course. You would go from January to June, and you would get your certificate if you had completed the work that was given. I was in bookkeeping, and whatever else I was doing, I was very good at it.

A Testimony of Healing

But before the end of the term I took deathly sick. This was still in back of the store where we had church. When they saw it looked like I wasn't going to live, they did call the doctor, but they weren't doctor-oriented. The doctor said, "She's very sick," and it sounded like they might have said I had tuberculosis or something. "She's got to get out of the house," they said, because of the others in the house. What I had was not going to be good for the family.

My mother came to me and she said, "Well, Hattie, they said you'll have to go out of house to the hospital [or wherever they were going to send me]. If you don't want to go, I'm not going to insist, but it is up to you because you are old enough now to say if you want to go or not."

And I said, "Mama, if I am going to live or die, I'm the Lord's. I don't care, it doesn't matter, I would like to stay home."

So she said, "I just want to know. If you want to stay here, Mama is going to pray." And she went in the basement, because we were the janitors of the house anyway; she prayed, and I guess she told the Lord not to take me away, because then she had lost two children, and this would be the next one.

People would come in to visit, to see how I was. Many of them, because of my frail body, they'd say, "Is she still alive? Is she living or dead?" They were just questioning. Now my body was so frail I became delirious. I really was out. If you came to visit me and you told me when I was alert, "I came to see you last night, but you didn't say so much," I'd say, "Nobody came to see me last night." And people would say, "What's wrong with you? I did come." My skin, my hair, everything just peeled.

Priscilla wired my father and told him, "Mama has Hattie here dying, and she is going to be the next one." My little sister was gone, and they were all worried that Mama was going to sit there and let Hattie die. He was pastoring in Rochester, New York. He came down to Brooklyn, and he said, "Now, my God, I got to think about who's going to preach her funeral, what to do, how to carry on."

By that time, a break had come to my body and I was beginning to mend. And he said, "I know they were keeping something back from me. But they had stars on it." And they said when they had stars on a telegram that meant death, and he was so sure. But when he came home, he saw me in bed—I was lying, not up—and he went to the kitchen and asked my mother how I was. No, first he had asked me, and I said, "I'm all right."

My father was a great Sunday-school man, a great teacher. He had been planning a Sunday-school convention in Rochester, and I wanted to go. And he knew I was too sick to come. He said, "No, you can't go there."

And that's what made him go in the kitchen and ask Mama; maybe he thought I was really sick. He said, "Missy [that's what he called my mother], how is that girl?"

She said, "Well, she is of age, ask her."

He shook his head and didn't know what to do with any of us then. He said, "Now girl, how are you?"

I said, "I want to go to the convention."

He got so sick of me! He said, "What is the matter?" The telegram had got him really down. And here I am wanting to come to the convention. *What is this?* The Lord had touched my body; the crisis now was over. And I began to mend.

At that time I had just been elected for New York State Church of God Youth president, and I would be the youngest one they had ever had. Brother George Clark and I and several others had gone to Far Rockaway, and we started the New York State Youth Convention. We had a lovely organization, but I took sick so bad. I was so sick they thought I wasn't going to be here, but the convention went on, even though I had to stay home.

I finally got better, well enough to go to the Board of Health. I couldn't go back to my job. I worked for the Bureau of Taxation and

Assessment, but I couldn't go to school or do nothing. Before I could go anywhere to be around people, I had to go to the Board of Health and get a final checkup from the doctor. And so I did, and everything worked out: I was OK, I was well.

That was one episode, my sickness. One of the brothers, Brother Yearwood, came to my bed, one of the nights that looked like I was really gone out. He said, "Oh, no, Hattie can't die. God's got a work for her to do." And that aroused my insides. His saying that was something that shook me up inside: *God has a work for you to do.* Well, no one had said anything about my having anything to do for God. God looked like he didn't need me, because I had nothing to offer. It wasn't that night, but after that it seemed like I began to pick up mending and mending and mending.

Now I remember very well when my mother took me to the doctor after I had no blood, I was just dried up. There was nothing happening to my body. I had to learn to walk. I had gone blind; my sight had gone. And it was a matter of having patience with me. My mother was very patient, but she knew the Lord had healed me, and she would thank the Lord for healing me. But when we went to the doctor, the doctor examined me carefully. He said, "Well, there's nothing wrong with you." He told my mother, "The only thing that could happen to a girl at this age, she'd either have to be in decline [which meant tuberculosis] or expecting."

Now, he told my mother that away from me; he didn't let me hear him say that, she told me. And I got very angry with him. My mother asked the doctor what to do. He gave her a prescription for beef, iron and wine. He said, "Now this will snap her back."

And my mother said, "If you just hadn't said wine." This is my mother's mentality for God and for Jesus, because she had never had any wine, and the man said, "Give her beef, iron and wine." And that's in a bottle; that was the name of the medicine at that time. If he just hadn't said the wine, she would have bought it. But she prayed, "Lord, give me what to do for my child." And the Lord gave her a prescription. She got beets and blackberries and grape juice. The beets were cooked until after they turned white, all the blood was out, and the blackberries crushed and mashed. And she made it in a bottle, and I had to take that every so many hours. I wasn't eating too much, because I was an avid eater when I was able to eat—that's how people knew I was sick, when I didn't eat, because this was the eater! When she did that for me I got better, got well and started to get fat, and I said, "Oh, Mama, I'm getting too big."

And she says, "No, we asked the Lord to heal you. Don't you touch nothing. Don't you say anything. The Lord is healing you and you have nothing to do with it."

I said, "Yes, but I didn't want to be a fatted calf."

Listening for the Call

The Lord touched me, I got healed, and I was ready to go again. And then that which Brother Yearwood had said started worrying me. And I asked my mother, "Mama, how does a person know when he is called of God or when he wants you to do something?" She said, "Well, if you're available. If you are available and commit your life, the Lord will call you because you are ready to go."

So I started, not knowing what all this means, but I said to myself one day he might want me to do something, because I had already gotten that deep down in me that somebody said the Lord had something for me to do. So I wanted to know, how do you get to do what the Lord's will is?

World War II: Work in Washington, D.C.

In later years, after high school, I took the civil service tests for clerk-typists and I did finally land a job in Washington, D.C. But I had taken the test so many times my sister-in-law, my brother Joe's wife, said, "You still taking tests?"

And I said, "Oh, yes, I'm going to take the test until I pass it—I don't care how long it takes. One day I'll get a job." Some I saw were so depressed and had nothing, and they looked so bad, and then there were some that came who looked like they had some type of profession and they were coming with a newspaper in their hand and they looked like they had accomplished something. And I said, "I want to be like that—I want to have something to look forward to."

In 1942, in February, after the war started, I was called to Washington. The time came for me to go to Washington. I went to Manhattan to the Church of God on 129th Street; the late Reverend H. E. Green was the pastor. Even though he was the senior minister in the city of New York, we young people went to him for advice and prayer. The first thing he would do when you got to him was "Let us pray." And he prayed for me. I explained to him and told him about what I was about, that the Lord had allowed me to get this job in Washington and I wanted to pray. So we prayed.

And I went to Washington to work, not knowing very many people there. I knew the Church of God at Third Street; I knew Pansy Brown and several others. I went to live with a woman on Isherwood Street, on the east side. I stayed in that home. After a while I wasn't too pleased living in the living room, because they were crowded down there. So Sister Juanita Duncan of the Church of God, who didn't live too far from the church, let me live in her home. I had a room with Sister Duncan. I lived there until I got called out of that work altogether.

All this time, in 1942, I was working in the church with the children of the Church of God. By this time my family had moved from 21 Sumter Street, our original place where we lived, to 1608 Bergen Street. And right across the street, the Sumter Street Mission had moved to another storefront, 1611 Bergen Street. So that's where we were. My mother still was the founder and pastor.

I was settled now, but for a few weeks I was coming back home because I had never been away from home before, and I was frightened. Two things frightened me: living away from home was bad enough, but having to work at night was worse. They had shifts in Washington at that time.

When in Washington I was working for the Treasury Department, but it was to count money. I was in the Bureau of Engraving and Printing. We counted old money that had been returned to be destroyed. Now, that was a job that didn't give you a break. At night you would be working and working, and they would almost call you into question if you went to the bathroom. Now, I am learning how to be assertive, and I went to the head of the department. Two other girls went with me, and I asked them why couldn't we get a break to go and rest a minute. Counting this money was very taxing. So they took the grievance, and after a while we got a ten-minute break twice during the course of a day. So we did do something about it.

Chicago

I wasn't in Washington a whole year. The job moved to Chicago. And the government helped us to move. They moved us, and we went to Chicago in a Pullman. Everything was paid and taken care of. You didn't have very much expense or anything. Brother and Sister Cooper lived in Chicago. They were great friends of ours, and they have a daughter named Elizabeth. They moved to Chicago, and I lived with them. His job with the Railroad Retirement Board moved them up to Chicago from Washington at the same time we moved. I lived on Langley Avenue, about a couple of blocks from the Langley Avenue Church of God at 62nd and Langley. At first I started worshiping at the Langley Avenue Church of God, but then Sister and Brother Cooper went to the church at 63rd and May. The church has moved twice since then. I worshiped all those years there. I was very happy working with them as an usher and youth counselor, anything I could do, because I was in Chicago. And because I was a person that had worked in the church all my life, I was glad to be there at the church.

We stayed in Chicago from 1942 to 1945, when I gave up the job. In fact it was just as well, because a little after I gave up the job the war was over. I had quite a bit of experience during the war years, though. There was a shortage of everything. You had to stand in line for everything, for sugar and for shoes and for gas if you had a car, and for stockings. I can remember ladies being in line out the store and way down to the corner trying to get a pair of nylon stockings. Everybody had runs. It didn't look bad, because you didn't have stockings. I always wore dresses a little longer than everybody else, so they would tell me I didn't support the war effort. Everybody was supposed to wear short clothes. I wore my dresses like I wanted to.

Hearing the Call

I had a very good experience working in Washington and Chicago. I worked in Chicago in the Merchandise Mart, and I was promoted. They called it promoted, but they just upgraded my title and gave me a little more salary. I became a clerk with two typists. I would be the examiner, so they raised my salary a little bit.

I had helped in the beginning of the Youth Convention, which started in Chicago right before the war. And it was going nicely in the first few years. The war was on, and they said no travel. You couldn't get vacation time during the winter because they said no travel. So that meant stay home, but I was on the program, and I felt that I should be there. Everybody had to cancel anything they had said about going away, and if they had offered or said anything about vacation, everything was canceled.

Seems as if I was bold enough, because nobody thought that this timid little Christian woman would ever do that; I was supposed to be so quiet and demure. But I said, "I have to go to this meeting." So I went up to wherever the supervisor of the supervisors was, and we had a talk.

"Why do you have to go?"

I said, "I am a part of a youth convention, and we are trying hard to help the young people stay in school, or whatever." I was telling them about the times in which we lived, that I had an assignment, and it was very important that I be at this meeting.

And some of the people in this big office where all these people were working in mass production said, "You ain't going to get nowhere. You know everybody that went up there they said no to."

So I didn't say anything. And when I didn't want to talk, I was praying, and I wasn't letting no one hinder me from praying, so I wasn't arguing back with people to tell me what couldn't be done, because I said in my heart that I was going to someone higher than the man I had to talk to.

So when I went up to him and got through my little speech telling him why I had to go, he said, "Listen, you can go, but you be back the day after New Year's Day. Don't be absent and don't be late."

I didn't hesitate to tell him I'd be back with flying colors, or whatever. I said, "I'll be back."

He said, "You go downstairs and say nothing to anybody. But you are getting permission to go, that's an understanding, as long as you will be back at your desk at the right time."

Whew! I went downstairs and I wanted to holler, "Praise the Lord," and all like that, and I wasn't as open and verbal as I am now. I would have hollered "Praise God" right before the man then, but I was sort of quiet. I can remember now how dumb I was—I didn't talk at all. I have learned now to open my mouth wide and talk.

I went to this convention, it was in St. Louis. And I was showing slides on boy-girl relationships. Oh, my. The Lord blessed the meeting. Brother Gabriel Dixon was an able pastor, one of our great young men at that time. We had a wonderful time. I'll never forget that meeting, because I know how the Lord had helped me to overcome a hurdle. That gives you faith to believe if God can do that, so why worry about anything else? So when they found out that I was going, it wasn't until I came back; they didn't see me on the job. But the Lord blessed anyway: I went to the convention and came back and I had something to talk about.

Now the same youth convention was meeting in Brooklyn, New York, in 1944, at the Christmas convention. At that time we didn't meet in hotels and big places. We just met in churches. We were growing, but we weren't a big convention. And the saints that came from afar were housed in homes. So that's the way that convention was in 1944. Louise Terry and several others were the leaders at that time. She was the president.

We were praying, and the war was still going strong. In 1944 it wasn't over yet. They were still hurling the bombs and shooting people down. So they were praying that the Lord would give someone to go and work with the young people. This was at the Lafayette Avenue Church of God in Brooklyn. Reverend Evans Marshall was the pastor. This must have been one of the first times I had stayed up all night. It was an all-night prayer, that they were trying to find someone who was going to be that person to go and work with the young people and encourage them.

And I don't know what possessed me, because at that time I was almost ready to say that I did not understand how God speaks to people. Like Samuel—he didn't understand that it was the Lord speaking to him. But I got up off my knees early in the wee hours of that morning and said, "I'll be that person to go in the field."

This was in December. They gave me a chance to get ready to tell my job I was leaving. And in August of that year I was to tell them that I was going to leave the job to go work in the field. So they thanked the Lord: "Sister Hattie Downer is going to be that person."

And I was kind of slow in knowing how and what I was doing because, like Abraham, I really had no experience of how I was going to do, or what I was going to do, but I was going to be the field worker.

Commissioned

They had what we called a Field Worker Committee. That was Brother Vivian Hudson, Sister Elizabeth O'Neal and Sister Louise Terry. They were going to plan an itinerary for me and start me out working for God through the country. That part was what made me feel, *Now that you have opened your mouth, you've got to go through with it.* You just don't say things like that. Because if the Lord is for you to go, you've got to go.

So January, February, March, April, May, June—now I had to tell them I was leaving the job in July. And I wouldn't be back. When I had to tell them that, the man—the supervisor—asked me, "Well, Miss Downer, are you leaving this job for another job, a better job?"

And I said, "I think so."

"Where are you going?"

At that time, when we young colored children got a job, that was very important, because you don't get jobs easily. And there's no other jobs out there. People wondered what did I mean by saying I was going to a better job, but in my heart I said, *If I could help a young person to find a better life, I think it would be paying me more than dollars and cents.*

That supervisor said, "Is it paying more money?" So that was my answer, to say if I felt like a young person was finding a better way of life that would be to me more than dollars and cents.

So they all said, "She's out of her mind. So what? Let her go." They were very shocked and surprised, but I really meant it, and when the time came I had to give up the job. And that August at camp meeting, they called me and they laid hands on me and prayed God's blessing upon the work that I had to do. And I had to travel. This was starting the traveling for the work of the Church of God throughout the country.

Doing the Work of God in the Field

I worked from 1945 to 1955 in the field, approximately ten years. I'd come in and out. I'd come home, but I lived in the suitcase. During those years the committee called me in because they needed a well on the campground at West Middlesex, Pennsylvania. So they stopped the field work for a season, for some weeks or months, or whatever, and they gave me an itinerary to go to the churches all over the country in the North and West. I went as far as Indiana, Ohio, Michigan, New York, New Jersey and Pennsylvania. I can remember these different churches—some churches I went to two in a day, maybe three in a day if they had me to go somewhere at night. This was for the campaign to get funds. We would get pledges to raise funds for the well. They didn't give me any money hardly, because anything they gave me I had to send in because they needed the money so desperately to help get the well. But they did get the well.

My field work took me to many places all over the country. In the work of the Lord, you just don't know where you're going. The first real trip in my field work to go out of the state of New York was in Junction City, Kansas, at the youth convention that was to be held there. Carfare from Brooklyn to Manhattan was a dime on the subway. But I had so much packing, so many packages, and my little pocketbook slipped under my arm, it either dropped or someone took it. It had all my money in it, my ticket and everything. I was on my way to the Penn Station, and I didn't know what to do. So when I sat down on the subway and I found out I didn't have my pocketbook, I said, *I must go back to check and see how I lost it.* So I came back, and I went home. It was just something that happened, and I must say, it might have fallen from under my arm, since I was so packed with things. All I had was that dime in my hand to put in the slot. I had taken off my watch and I had taken all my money and I had done all the work that I had to do at home. I left everything straightened out, I thought.

And when I came back home, I didn't know what to do because my mother wasn't home. And I just had to say a prayer. But right away I called the committee to let them know I didn't have my ticket. They wired the ticket back to me right away. "They're looking for you at this meeting, so you have to go."

So I went on, but I didn't have any money now, just the ticket. I didn't have any pocketbook or nothing. I was frightened now: *Lord, what to do?* But I said, *Since I have to go, they emphatically said you had to be at this place, they are looking for you, so don't disappoint them.* So I did go. I changed trains in Chicago. And I began to pray, because I can't sleep, I don't have any food. I said, *Lord, please explain to me what I'm doing. I don't know.* And then the Lord—we are on good terms, but I haven't been that close to him, because me and him haven't been on speaking terms like I'm intimate with him and like people "hear from heaven" all like that. I didn't know anything. Poor little pitiful woman. And the Lord spoke to me just as nice and said, "Now you're trusting the Lord."

I had thought, *I'm going on faith, I'm going on with the Lord's work, and I'm just tickled to death that I'm working for God.* He said, "Now, you're going on faith. You've got nothing. And you're looking forward to nothing." And may I explain that I don't know where I'm going, for I have no addresses in my pocketbook. And I'm on the train and I'm thinking about this now. So I know I am going to Junction City, Kansas, and it is a one-horse town. It's built up now, but way back then you got off the train and the train kept going.

They just dumped you, and it's midnight. But the Lord has always taken care if you're doing his will. I got that from my mother, if you're in His will He will take care of you. He's not going to leave you stranded.

I got to the station. Got off with my luggage. The man had put my luggage on the ground, on the station platform. And I'm standing there, and here comes a man with a cab. And he says, "Where do you want to go?"

I said, "I don't know, but I know I have to go to Sister Parr."

"Oh, everybody knows Sister Parr. Come on, let's go." Just like that. He knows Sister Parr, and all I've got to do is go in the cab and let him take me to Sister Parr.

And I said, "Well, thank the Lord." And I got in the cab and I began to tell him. I didn't tell him I didn't have no money, because I was scared he might put me out. I said, "You know Sister Parr?"

He said, "Everybody knows her. She's the one woman in this town that everybody knows; she is everybody's friend."

So we got to Sister Parr's house. Gabriel Dixon and the saints were at Sister Parr's house praying for me to get there safely. This is the night after the meeting started. When the man put my suitcase on the porch, I said, "Hold it just a minute, please. Let me go inside."

And I said, "Saints, I lost my pocketbook. I don't have any money to pay this man. So would you please just give me enough to pay him so he can go?" So they did—I think it was one or two dollars. And I gave it to the man, and he thanked me, and he went about his business.

And they began to praise the Lord, and "Sister Hattie is here" and all that. And these people didn't know me, see. Here are some people who don't know a thing about me, never seen me before. I didn't mean too much to them. But after that night I meant a lot to them and they meant a lot to me.

So I took Brother Gabriel aside and explained to him what had happened, and he said, "Sister Downer, don't worry about nothing, you're OK, you're taken care of. God is going to bless you. Why don't you just go ahead and think about what you've got to do?"

Well, being a young recruit, I didn't know too much. I was mostly like Abraham who really didn't know what he was doing, but he was going because God said it. And that's really what I was doing. Before the meeting was out, Brother Gabriel had a special offering, and I know the collection was more than I'd had in my pocketbook. So that part, monetarily, didn't affect me really at all. It was just a matter of a few worldly things I had in there to lose and give up. But the Lord had helped me through that. And we had a good meeting.

After Junction City, I went to Topeka, I went to every place in Kansas—Kansas City, Kansas; Kansas City, Missouri; and two or three other places. Whenever I'd go in a state, I worked the whole state. No matter where I went, the Lord had some young people that I can see today, grown men and women, working for God vigorously.

We taught and we preached. With children and young people we had flannelgraphs. We had classes in boy-girl relationships. We had talks to the parents. Some nights I had to give the message for the pastor. Many of the nights young people gave their hearts to the Lord, in all places.

I was in Atlanta, Georgia, in the forties. I remember the night when we had worked so hard there in the church, with the children in the day and with the parents at night. We were talking and working with the altar and working with the children, and it looked like I had spent my life—the Lord had used every bit of it, every ounce of strength I had physically, and I was just talking on, like supernatural, whatever. The Lord had taken me out of myself. And I went in the office, and I just threw myself over exhausted. But the Lord had done a beautiful job with the young people that night in Atlanta, Georgia. And here emerges one of the finest pastors in our congregations, Brother Rudolph Smith.

I worked in Chicago, and in Detroit. I lived with one Sister Marie Jones in Detroit. I would go to different places; they had a lot of churches in Detroit. Sister Marie Jones was always my headquarters; I'd come back and I'd have a foothold. I went to Lansing. It was cold when I went to Lansing, and I worked with a brother from the South. When I worked in the Ohio area, I lived with Brother and Sister Hudson in Dayton; that was like headquarters. Springfield, Xenia, Cincinnati, Columbus and

Hamilton—I worked all those churches, and then my stationary place would be Dayton. I would go back and forth mostly by bus to all these different places. When I had to go far, I would go by train. I went Pullman most of the time; I had a roomette.

I went through the state of Georgia and had different cities—Dublin, Easton, Statesboro, Augusta—several cities like that where I worked in places. And when I got to Statesboro, they had a business meeting. The pastor didn't come but once a month, so they didn't want anybody else coming in. But one of the ladies said, "She came to help us with the children, so we will have her come in and do it."

Well, the week we were there, the Lord blessed us. The school opened up; I talked to the children in public school. And that brought the children out to church. And they had a much better audience for the work that I was doing than they would have had for the church work. So they all were quite surprised about that. But they didn't understand that they needed somebody to help them with the work.

And a lot of times I might have gotten discouraged, but the Lord blinded my eyes to everything they were doing to me. I'm talking about it now like it was fun, because I didn't see the malice or whatever you would call it—I don't have words to underscore it. But I didn't understand nothing like *they're mad or they don't want me, or they this, that and the other.* I just thanked the Lord that I had an opportunity to share, because a lot of times I have been places like in Kansas where some lady said, "Oh, I wish that I could do what you're doing for God. You seem to be doing a great job for the Lord." And she had three or five children.

I said, "Do you know, the Lord has blessed you to do a better job than I? Look what you have. You have produced fine children. And the Lord wants you to serve them and make them very good children. Teach them the way of the Lord. You have a lot to do. What I'm doing is what God wants me to do. But what he has provided you right here, he has given you your work, cut it out for you. So you must do what the Lord wants you to do."

She said, "I never thought of it like that." And we went and we had good services.

I remember Statesboro so well, how the Lord blessed the work there because the school opened the door and told the children that we would be at the Church of God. And it was an interesting time we had.

I did a lot of work with the children with the flannelgraph, and that was the closest I could get with them. I had the filmstrips, but some of the pastors didn't want me to show them. But the flannel-graph they didn't bother. You run into a lot of conservatism and narrow-mindedness when you work in the church work.

But a lot of places had no restraint on whatever I did. In fact, some wanted to change their curriculum, but I told them, "No, you can't do anything unless your pastor preaches it. You are living under a pastor. I am only coming here with ideas and suggestions, but I don't change nothing the pastor doesn't agree to." But a lot of the pastors were very happy with some of the things that we were initiating, and it was good for the youth and the church.

Church of God Board of Home Missions

When I started out with the committee from the National Associa-tion of the Church of God in West Middlesex, Pennsylvania, in August 1945, I went from this congregation to that congregation with whatever they gave me. The churches would see that I got what I got. I had nothing given to me from West Middlesex, nothing. I was asked to do a job in South Carolina for the Church of God Board of Home Missions in Anderson, Indiana, and they got me the office and they had no field workers. In fact, I was the only field worker the Church of God had, white or black, while I was working for the National Association. But the board at Anderson asked if I could work for Sister Mattie McGee, who had asked for help. She was the woman who worked at the State College in Orangeburg, but she was a state leader of South Carolina youth. Her work was important. She asked them to allow someone to come and help them. So they got ahold of me.

Well, I got the committee to say if I could go or not. And they were very reluctant. They always felt that they got something now and somebody wanted to take it, like I would be taken from them to go to Anderson. But that wasn't the case. In this case it was our people helping our people. They gave me all the books and all the literature I needed to help me. I was going to work with women, children, youth, the whole bit. But my main purpose was going down there organizing Daily Vacation Bible School. So I got released to do that. But it was field work too. But in the meantime, when they asked me to come to do that, they thought about compensation at that time. So knowing that I wasn't being compensated by the national work, they suggested giving me something for the work that I was doing. But then it continued after I had finished my assignment in South Carolina. What they were giving me continued to be what I would get. But I kept working. I worked in Columbia, Sumter and Orangeburg, South Carolina. And we had some very important days together down there. The saints worked with the children, and I worked with the older ones in the evenings, and we had very, very enjoyable times together.

When I was in North Carolina, I worked Chapel Hill with Brother C. T. Boyd and his family. It was during the time of polio, which was infantile paralysis. The powers that be said no public assembly because the polio was so bad. So we couldn't have the Vacation Bible School; we couldn't have anything at church. I want to make the point of how important the flannelgraph was to my work. Sister Minnie Davis had a big family of boys and girls. On their lawn we had Vacation Bible School with the neighborhood children and their children. We had a very enjoyable time teaching them from the flannelgraph, and that helped to enhance what I was trying to do. We had no problem; we had singing, the same things that we would do at any other place we did with them. It was very well done, and the Lord blessed. We worked with children that are still in the Church of God.

I went to Mississippi and Louisiana. We worked with Ozie Wattleton in Louisiana. Ozie and Olita Burnett (Fontenot) and myself went to Louisiana together. I will never forget Sister Olita Burnett. After she graduated from high school, she prayed and asked God, "What now, next for my life?" And Sister Ozie had a plan ready to go to Oak Grove to start a new work in that area. We didn't know anybody—no souls, no nothing. But we hired a house, we got in the house, and the three women worked together. And I went to church early because I worked with the children, and then they did the preaching at night. No matter what weather, it was terrible weather there. When it got wet in Louisiana, it was like rubber, your foot was pulling rubber, and it rained a lot.

And one night, when we thought it wouldn't be nothing, they said, "Well, Sister Hattie, you go on to church, and we'll be on later." And I said I didn't think anybody was going to come anyway. But we went, and that night we had the biggest crowd. The Lord blessed and saved souls, and one of the men that got saved was a professor or principal in a school, and he gave his heart to the Lord. It was amazing: he gave his heart to the Lord first, and then his wife gave her heart to the Lord.

We had a tent meeting, and under that tent souls came. And Ozie was a marvel, the way God used her to bring souls out of sin and confusion. She just spoke from the book of Acts about the New Testament church of God, and she just used that as her theme, and she went through and just ripped up anything that wasn't true, because she's that type of preacner. But she did a job for God, and the Lord saved souls. And we left a church there. It wasn't long before a little church was erected too. When I left, I left Ozie and Olita there. Olita became the pastor of Oak Grove, Louisiana.

I went to New Orleans, away from Sister Olita and Sister Ozie. Brother Burns, the pastor, asked me to come and work with his group. A little after that—it had to be in the middle fifties—my father called me and said my mother was sick. Everybody had gone from home, and the rest of them had their families, and nobody was home to help with my mother. So he asked me to come home, and I was so sorry, because I was enjoying Louisiana. But I had to leave.

When I left and came home, my mother had been sick, but the Lord healed her, and she started in 1955 what we called the Williamsburg work. We started in a tiny little storefront with boys and girls. And when I got home, she said, "Hattie, I have put up a tent and I want you to help to run it." She put the tent up, and we kept the tent up from July to November.

And then in November or December I went to California. In my field work I stopped in Omaha and Lincoln, Nebraska. I went on to Colorado, I went to where Brother Emory Williams's wife was from, Denver. When I went to California, I went up and down the state, to Hanford and Oakland. I worked with white and black churches during that time when I was there. And I had some very lovely times with the saints in California. And I liked it out there because it was such sweet weather in December. I was telling the children it was snowing, and the boys and girls in New York were having fun on sleds and things (because it snowed in those years more heavily than it does now). And they would say they wished they were there, and I would say in my heart, *I'm so glad I'm here!* It was so nice out there.

In Texas someone was so concerned about my being single. They said, "Sister Hattie, have you ever been married?"

And I said, "No, nobody but to Jesus, and when I marry again."

And when I said "when I marry again," that worried her. She said, "She said 'marry again'? Who was she married to? When did she get married?"

Well, that did it. I never had so much fun. I said, "No, my husband is Jesus. I haven't had any more than that." But I had a very good time in Texas, in San Antonio and in all those little towns in between.

Storefront Missions in Brooklyn

I came in from California, and this time I came in to stay with my mother. Mother had pastored 1611 Bergen Street, where we moved from the first to that place. That was when I went to Washington to work. My mother had moved to 9 Columbus Place. I bought a car in 1955 or 1956, but I had stopped traveling. I was going back and forth to storefront missionary meetings. My mother had given up the work at Bergen Street, and she was opening up this little place on Moore Street in Williamsburg—that's where the storefront church was. We worked there with the children. My mother erected this tent, and I served under the tent and got the children church-orientated, because there were three children who had never been to church.

Many a parent came down after we had taught them, and they said the children were learning and they didn't know, so they came down. We had some mothers get saved through the work going up and down the stairs, recruiting the people like that. And the work of the Lord prospered.

Before we closed the tent down, we would get people to come and help us. Brother and Sister Terry from Plainfield, New Jersey, would come and cooperate with us. We didn't have too many in the New York area to help us at this time. But we began to get Puerto Ricans to come in, because they were beginning to come in a great number to New York. My mother was concerned about them, so the Church of God New York helped her send for Sister Bacquie in Cuba. She was from Jamaica, but she had been in Cuba; most of her children were born in Cuba. She came and took over the Spanish work. And it was beautiful. One of our first converts was a Spanish person in our church at that time. We had quite a group coming in and out.

Then we moved to 105 Knickerbocker Avenue. We had this day camp that the government helped sponsor. We had funds to run it very well. We did a good job. We had a bookkeeper and a secretary and a supervisor. We got money to pay the workers, and the city gave us what we called the youth coworkers. They gave us young people to work from the age group fourteen to twenty-one. The city paid for them. Now this was in the sixties. The first person to come to work for us from Anderson was Tabitha Meyer. She had an accordion, she had tracts, and she was like the Pied Piper. We got children of all ages and sizes, and it was a blessing. Then the next year they sent us two or three more students, what they called "Tri-S" students, from Anderson. [Tri-S is a summer student service program at Anderson University; the name means "study, serve and share."] We would get students every year, and we got them for about six years, children coming back and forth from Anderson College to Brooklyn.

And we got the city to help the children. Brooklyn College had a program for children that were trying to get into college but weren't prepared, called Upward Bound. Our church was one of those stations that recruited them and helped them to get prepared to take the SAT. We were one of the churches that sponsored that along with the students from Brooklyn College. And one of the ladies, DeVera Johnson—she has passed now—was very instrumental in helping us get students updated so they could matriculate into college.

We had people who were very interested in the work, and the Lord blessed. One of the finest people who came to help was Sue Miller, daughter of Brother T. Franklin Miller, who was then the chief man on the Board of Christian Education in Anderson. Sue Miller was a very, very middle-class white, and she came to New York in Brooklyn in the slums, and she was transformed. Her father and mother said, "Nothing has done any good for that girl until she went to New York. She came back a different person." She was a great guide. She and several others came. Most all the kids that came were white, except just one or two were black. I can't say too much for any of them, because they did tremendously well.

We had a thrift shop where the children could come and get clothing. We had a recreation center where they could come and have games and just have recreation. We rented three storefronts at the same time, on Varron Street, McKinnon Street and the one on Knickerbocker Avenue, the church center. We worked with mothers and fathers who did community work. Sometimes we would ask the children to come after school. We had a public school teacher to come and teach them during the day camp. She was upgrading the children. In the mornings we would ask them to come by; we would give them cocoa and a danish for breakfast.

Our work started breakfast in the public school in our community, because we were giving the children breakfast, and the children would be late going to school, because they came by the church first. And they wanted to know why they were late. But it gave me an opportunity to see how they were going to school. Some were going to school not cleaned up at all. Some had torn pockets, torn buttons, and I had needle and thread. I didn't do this alone, because some brothers and sisters used to come over from Jamaica in the morning to help me get these kids straightened out so they could go to school looking properly. We had one little white boy that got up in the morning—he was just as filthy and dirty as the little black children. And I said, "Now look, I don't want this. You're a little white boy. You are supposed to be clean." We had to have a washcloth there ready to wash his face and hands. And clean up children. We did everything for them.

Then we taught them that you have to not only come to school clean, but you have to love the Lord with a clean heart. We taught them the things that they should know about the Lord. And for the parents, we'd call them in to have meetings with them concerning the neighborhood. We didn't call it block associations then, but we got from the government—Mayor John Lindsay's administration way back—we got money to paint stoops, to make our community look better. And we got a citation for that, for having done some of the work in the community. And the parents were sharing this with us.

A Building for Urban Missions: The Cathedral of Joy
In 1973 my mother passed. In June of 1974 I got the building on George Street. When I passed this building, which I had been passing every day for all the years we were going to that storefront on Knickerbocker Avenue, the Spirit of the Lord stopped me and said, "Stop the car." And I stopped the car.

Next he said, "Get out the car." And I got out the car. And when I got out of the car and the car was in the street, he said, "Get on your knees and thank the Lord for this building."

And I said, "Well, Lord, this looks very foolish, but because I believe it is the voice of God, I will get on my knees." And I got on my knees on a stone step on a building that was so huge that I didn't even know how big it was, because I didn't look down the street, I just was there near the corner. I just got on my knees and said, "Thank you, Lord, for this building."

And then I went to church—this was on a Sunday morning—and I began to tell Emma Davis and I said, "Emma, guess what? I was stopped in my tracks to thank God for this building."

She said, "Sister Hattie, go teach your Sunday-school class." She didn't think I was right, so I didn't have a chance to tell her.

I went to Anderson and told Brother Tom Smith. He said, "Well, Hattie, I want to ask you something. Who told you about this building?"

I said, "I don't know, no one, I haven't seen anybody, but I believe the Spirit of the Lord wants us to have this building. Now I'm not sure. It may be just a building because they were telling me to look around to find a place for us to relocate from this spot where we were. Maybe this is what the Lord wants us to have, either to buy or whatever."

So he said, "Well, you find out some more about it, and when you come back to Anderson, tell us next year what you're doing." They weren't going to get excited over it with my not knowing anything. And I'm as excited as I could be.

I came back home, but I couldn't get that out my system, because I had to pass the building every day now from now on, and I had to find out who owned this building. They had a caretaker across the street around the corner, and I asked the man, "Do you know who owns the building across the street?"

And he said, "Yes."

I said, "Would you give me the phone number so I could call him up?"

He gave me the phone number and I called him. I said, "Is that building on George Street for rent?"

And he said, "Yes."

I said, "How much?"

He said, "Quote me a price."

I said, "Fifty thousand?"

The building was worth over $750,000. He said, "Yeah, I'll give it to you for fifty thousand dollars."

So I said, "OK." And I went to church and I told these people of the mission—they don't have fifty dollars hardly—and they said, "Sister Hattie, you know we don't have that kind of money."

"All I want to know, the man asked me did I want the building, I just want to know if you say yes so I can tell him."

And they said, "Well, you can tell him anything, but we can't buy no building with no money."

So I said, "OK, we'll just tell the man we want the building."

So we did. I went back and I called him.

He said, "What are you going to do with the building?"

I said, "Well, we are overcrowded with children, and we want more programs, and we're trying to do something for the community youth, and we were hoping that we could get a larger place."

He wanted to know all about what I was doing. I told him where we were and how we were getting along. He said, "You know what? I don't believe you can pay me for that building. I'm going to give it to you. I'm going to give you that building."

I said, "What did you say?"

He said, "I said I was going to give it to you."

I said, "Do you mean it?"

"Yes, and if anyone asks you anything, just tell them my name is Nutman, and a nut gave you the building!" When he finished saying that, that was enough for me. But I wasn't quite satisfied, because it is a little dubious here. He said, "Do you have a lawyer?"

I said, "Oh yes."

He said, "You have your lawyer call me."

I said, "All right."

And before I left where I was, I called the lawyer—thank God he was in his office. I said, "Call Mr. Nutman right now, because he said something about giving us this building on George Street, sir, and I want to know what he's doing."

So he called him up immediately; he said, "I'm Mr. Bicini, the lawyer for Reverend Downer. And she wanted to know what this was about."

He said, "Yes, it's all right. I just wanted to know if she was legitimate." Because *I* wanted to know if *he* was! He said, "Is she all right?"

He said, "Oh yes, she's a preacher," and he gave my credentials to him. So then, between the lawyers now it's going to be settled, not with me. So that's where we are.

That was the beginning of something that I cannot explain, because everywhere I went and told somebody about what the Lord had done, people would get hysterical. But the final part came when we went in the building. The building had been vandalized terribly. There was only one spot in the building that could be used for service; it was a big room that had wallpapering. And we thought the wallpaper was torn, but it wasn't torn; it was just the design that looked like it was torn. And we didn't have too much lighting up there to see it. But we opened up and found out that we could have service in this area. It was the dining hall upstairs. The downstairs had to be taken care of.

Before we got in the building for services, my secretary, Sister Gladys Davis, and I went with the lawyer to Mr. Nutman's office in Forest Hills, in Queens. And there we signed the papers and got the deeds for the building. When that was taken care of, I asked Mr. Nutman, "Well, don't we owe you a dollar? Don't we owe you something? Shouldn't we give you something?"

He said, "No. Go ahead and clean up your neighborhood. This is all I require."

So we did. We went out of the office very satisfied and came back, and therefore we began to check and do what we could in the building.

Provision

I began to tell people about the building. One man came to put in the telephone, and I told him about the building. Another man came to do something else for us, and when he left he shook his head and said, "What? This building?" He brought back one hundred Bibles.

I had six teenagers working that summer. We hired them for the summer to get the building in order, because it was so vandalized—to clean it up. They did. I think they did a lot more vandalizing than they did cleaning up, but they were young people, and we just were glad that they could get money for the summer.

We went somewhere else to a hardware store, and I told the man about the building. We needed a pump in the basement to get the water out. He said, "I'm going to give you the pump."

I told a lady on the street, and she began to praise God speaking in tongues. I said, "Go ahead, help yourself." She was so happy to hear that. And I was so much excited about things.

So I went upstairs one day, and it seemed as if a cloud of depression came, because the enemy was trying to tell me, "Somebody's going to come in here and tell you to get out of this building. You know you can't have this building on terms like that."

And I started to get so disturbed, but the Spirit of the Lord came and jerked me and said, "Every place you step and put your foot in this building, up or down, is the Church of God, it's yours. Go ahead, it's yours."

So I came downstairs, and we had to get the rooms designated. There were a lot of rooms there. They had the salesmen's rooms, because it had been a warehouse for the Schlitz distributors. We fixed it up. We went down to see about getting tax exemption for this building. They sent a representative out to check it. So we only had the upstairs ready for service, and they said, "We can't exempt this building because it's not being used for the purpose you say. You said it was a church, but where's the church? You don't have nothing going like a church."

So that just did something to me. I said, "We've got to get this tax exemption, because if it isn't exempted we pay two thousand dollars every quarter for taxes."

So we had to do something. So the Spirit of the Lord got on me again and said, "Get everything moved downstairs immediately, the piano, seats and everything down there." So we had this downstairs area fixed up, all the rooms cleaned up and labeled. They weren't painted and fixed up nice, but they were labeled "Sunday School, Room No. 1," "Youth Department, Room No. 2," and upstairs the recreation and missionaries. Every room labeled, every room cleaned.

When the man came back, I said, "What do you think?"

He said, "Who helped you do this? When did you do all this?"

I pointed upstairs and said, "Jesus. God did it. What do you think?"

He said, "I'm not telling you anything; you just go back down in March [this was in November] and see what they say."

And when we went, this was a long, huge building, and it said,

"Entire building tax exempt." I praised God.

The Lord helped us to get everything straightened out. I wouldn't forget how the Lord helped us to get money to get the heat in the building. I was asking saints, different ones that I knew would help us, would they help us to get some money to fix it. And the money came in so quick and easy. We needed five hundred dollars to help us. And the Lord told me on the way to the post office, "Don't send out another letter."

Brother C. Milton Grannum was the pastor of High Street Church of God. And he and his saints came over to render service one Wednesday night. Their missionary president asked him if she could raise funds to help us. They didn't know what we needed. But that night when he preached, and when the saints finished their work, she presented to the church five hundred dollars from the High Street Church of God. That's all we needed.

So I said, "Well, Lord, let me get out your way and see what you're going to do, because I have nothing to do with this. Whatever is going on, it's up to you." But the Lord had a lot to do with it. I'm very pleased with what the Lord has done.

Suggestions for Further Reading

Clapp, Rodney. *Families at the Crossroads*. Downers Grove, Ill.: InterVarsity Press, 1993.

DeYoung, Curtiss Paul. *Coming Together: The Bible's Message in an Age of Diversity*. Valley Forge, Penn.: Judson, 1995.

Ellis, Carl F., Jr. *Free at Last? The Gospel in the African-American Experience*. Downers Grove, Ill.: InterVarsity Press, 1996.

Felder, Cain Hope. *Stony the Road We Trod: African American Biblical Interpretation*. Minneapolis: Fortress, 1991.

Fiorenza, Elisabeth Schüssler. *In Memory of Her: A Feminist Reconstruction of Christian Origins*. New York: Crossroad, 1983.

Hines, Samuel G., with Joe Allison. *Experience the Power*. Rev. ed. Anderson, Ind.: Warner, 1995.

Hoots, Allegra S., ed. *Prophetic Voices: Black Preachers Speak on Behalf of Children*. Washington, D.C.: Children's Defense Fund, 1993.

Keener, Craig S. *The IVP Bible Background Commentary*. Downers Grove, Ill.: InterVarsity Press, 1993.

Kroeger, Catherine Clark, Mary Evans and Elaine Storkey, eds. *Study Bible for Women: The New Testament*. Grand Rapids, Mich.: Baker Book House, 1995.

Leonard, Juanita Evans, ed. *Called to Minister, Empowered to Serve: Women in Ministry*. Anderson, Ind.: Warner, 1989.

Pannell, William. *The Coming Race Wars? A Cry for Reconciliation*. Grand Rapids, Mich.: Zondervan, 1993.

Perkins, Spencer, and Chris Rice. *More Than Equals: Racial Healing for the Sake of the Gospel*. Downers Grove, Ill.: InterVarsity Press, 1993.

Raboteau, Albert J. *Slave Religion: The "Invisible Institution" in the Antebellum South*. New York: Oxford University Press, 1978.

Sanders, Cheryl J. *Empowerment Ethics for a Liberated People*. Minneapolis: Fortress, 1995.

————. *Saints in Exile: The Holiness-Pentecostal Experience in African American Religion and Culture*. New York: Oxford University Press, 1996.

————, ed. *Living the Intersection: Womanism and Afrocentrism in Theology*. Minneapolis: Fortress, 1995.

Thurman, Howard. *Jesus and the Disinherited*. Richmond, Ind.: Friends United, 1949, 1981.

Tucker, Ruth A., and Walter Liefeld. *Daughters of the Church: Women and Ministry from New Testament Times to the Present*. Grand Rapids, Mich.: Academie/Zondervan, 1987.

Usry, Glenn, and Craig S. Keener. *Black Man's Religion: Can Christianity Be Afrocentric?* Downers Grove, Ill.: InterVarsity Press, 1996.

Womack, Anita Smith. *Listen to the Children*. Anderson, Ind.: Board of Christian Education of the Church of God, 1993.